THE
STEPS

Elodagh ♡

ABOUT THE AUTHOR

Dr Clodagh Campbell's passion and soul purpose is to help others. To help them find peace to live a happy, fulfilled life. To help them feel less alone by supporting and empowering them to lower the distress they are experiencing. To help them heal.

As a psychologist who cares deeply about helping people, Clodagh specialises in compassionately supporting and empowering individuals to care for themselves and to come home to themselves. Through this process, Clodagh encourages readers to give themselves permission to slow down amidst the busyness and overwhelm of life, so that they can acknowledge how they feel, physically, as well as emotionally and mentally, and consider what changes they can make in their lives to calm the chaos of their minds and to honour their emotional needs, their boundaries and themselves. Clodagh's work is incredibly transformative and healing, and something she longs to share more with the world.

Through her own deep healing journey, the years she has spent studying and researching the world of psychology, and the countless hours she has spent sitting with people in her therapy room, Clodagh strongly believes that it is possible to heal and live happier, more peaceful and fulfilling lives. Clodagh's work is grounded in science and her clinical learnings from her therapy room. She is loved by her social media followers, podcast listeners, readers and clients alike for her warm, compassionate and authentic approach to inner healing and inner peace. And Clodagh has made it her life's mission to help others achieve this peace. For this reason, writing *The Steps* was an obvious extension of this for Clodagh and for many years she envisioned offering this to the world, when the time felt right. That time is now.

THE
STEPS

TEN LESSONS FROM THERAPY
ON HEALING, FINDING CALM
AND CREATING
LASTING INNER PEACE

Dr Clodagh Campbell

GILL BOOKS

Gill Books
Hume Avenue
Park West
Dublin 12
www.gillbooks.ie

Gill Books is an imprint of M.H. Gill and Co.

© Dr Clodagh Campbell 2025

978 1 8045 8086 8

Designed by Sarah McCoy
Edited by Jane Rogers
Proofread by Gillian Fitzgerald-Kelly
Printed and Bound in the UK using 100% Renewable Electricity at CPI Group (UK) Ltd
This book is typeset in Baskerville.

The paper used in this book comes from the wood pulp of sustainably managed forests.

All rights reserved.
No part of this publication may be copied, reproduced or transmitted in any form or by any means, without written permission of the publishers.

This book is not intended as a substitute for the medical advice of a physician. The reader should consult a doctor or mental health professional if they feel it necessary.

A CIP catalogue record for this book is available from the British Library.

5 4 3 2 1

For my mum, my greatest teacher
and the one who taught me to love.

In loving memory of my father,
who I miss each and every day.

CONTENTS

Introduction 1
Step One Honour Your Emotions 5
Step Two Calm the Chaos of Your Mind 41
Step Three Regulate Your Nervous System 69
Step Four Heal Your Inner Child 101
Step Five Silence Your Inner Critic 125
Step Six Cultivate Compassion 153
Step Seven Strengthen Your Self-Worth 173
Step Eight Cultivate Connection 203
Step Nine Honour Your Boundaries 231
Step Ten Accept What Is 265
Conclusion 293
Mental Health Support Services 297
Select Bibliography 299
Acknowledgements 301

INTRODUCTION

Welcome to *The Steps*, I am so glad you have arrived. If you've found yourself here, it is no coincidence – you were led here for a reason. Perhaps it's finally time to give yourself this gift: the gift of calm, the gift of peace of mind, the gift of acceptance, the gift of deep inner healing.

This moment is a pivotal one for you. In this moment you are holding the key to transformation in the palm of your hands, the key to change, the key to living a happy and fulfilled life, the key to the life you have yearned for, for so long now.

For years I too yearned for inner peace. I too yearned for calm, I too yearned to heal the wounds and deep inner pain I carried that impacted how I viewed myself and the world around me. It is for this reason that I wrote this book, for you.

So dive in. Read my words and allow them to settle deep inside your soul. They will give you the gift of understanding yourself on a deeper level than you ever have before. They will give you the gift of learning to honour your emotions, of healing your wounded inner child, of silencing your inner critic and offering yourself the self-compassion that will change everything for you. They will also give you the gift of strengthening your self-worth, and seeing yourself as the lovable and loved person you truly are. They will help you to cultivate connection and allow your inner wisdom to guide your life in a way it has never done before. They will bring you acceptance, deep inner peace and a new way of being in the world – a world that is beautiful, joyful and safe.

Throughout this book I share nine beautiful guided meditations to support you on your healing journey. You'll find audio recordings of these meditations on my website www.thewellnesspsychologist.ie, in the Meditation section under the Resources tab, and I invite you to listen to these as you complete *The Steps*. I hope my words and my voice help you to settle into the moment and into yourself. Meditation is a very special part of my life that calms, soothes and heals my every woe. I hope by sharing this gift with you it can offer you this experience too.

I hope this book will become your new bedside bible, one you reach for time and again. When life feels hard. When you feel shaky in yourself. When your inner child is calling to you to soothe and embrace them. When you need to calm the chaos of your mind and quieten the fear, stress and overwhelm that many of us feel every day. When you need a hand to hold, to guide you to be less judgemental and more patient and loving towards yourself. Let *The Steps* be this for you. Let my voice guide you on a journey of deep inner healing, and one that is meaningful and long-lasting. Allow me to help you slow down.

Allow me to help you change your life.

I hope you enjoy the beautiful ten-step journey I am about to guide you on. Go at your own pace. There is nothing to rush or to force here. Trust the process and trust me as I guide you along this path. This is the work. This is the healing. This is the most important book you will read this year.

This is your new bedside bible, and these are: *The Steps*.

All my love,
Clodagh x

STEP ONE

HONOUR YOUR EMOTIONS

WAVES

Your emotions arrive like waves
Wrapping around your heart
Some slow and gentle
Some shocking, tearing you apart

You do your best to silence them
To bury them down deep
Yet still they bubble to the surface
Denying you your sleep

You battle them, you fight them
You fear all they possess
If only you could welcome them
And allow yourself some rest

For these waves are sent to guide you
To steer you and keep you safe
Messages from deep within
Soul whispers to embrace

So when they next wrap around you
Or come knocking at your door
Welcome them, allow them in
Sit with them along the shore

Surrender your heart to them
And find their meaning deep within
For these waves bear gifts and buoyancy
A chance to catch your breath
Before preparing for your next swim

It's 1989 and a much younger version of me is crying hysterically. I've fallen over and scraped my knee and I am inconsolable. Fat, salty tears stream down my face and my emotion is so intense that I'm struggling to catch my breath. My mother holds me to her chest, desperately trying to soothe me, 'Shhh, don't cry, it's okay, I've got you.' I hiccup as I look up at her and she sees all the emotion displayed on my face. 'You're so angry you fell and hurt yourself, and you're so sad that your knee hurts so much. My poor baby.' She rocks me and does all she can to calm both me and my pain.

So much is happening in my above remembering. Not only is my mother soothing my distress, she is responding to a deep need I have to be seen, heard and validated. She is also teaching me an invaluable lesson: picking up on the cues I am demonstrating to her, she mirrors the emotions I am experiencing. She tells me, 'You're so angry . . . you're so sad.' What a wonderful gift this is because this is how, as children, we learn to register and identify our emotions. Anger, sadness, fear, disgust, shame, surprise and of course joy and happiness. Not just that, but she is also signalling to me to dry my tears, 'Shhh, don't cry.' It is in these moments of connection that we are taught what it is we are feeling, the good, the bad and the ugly. I say 'the good, the bad and the ugly', because that's what we learn, isn't it? That while some emotions are glorious, some are negative; and that our tears should be dried, 'Shhh, don't cry.'

This isn't done out of badness or impatience; well, it most certainly wasn't in my mother's case, who was the most patient and loving mother you could wish for in life. She hated seeing my distress, so she wanted to soothe it, and in the process to soothe me and my tears. My wails were alarming, uncomfortable and distressing (not just for me, but also for her because she loved me so much and wanted to do anything within her power to soothe me as quickly as possible). I experience this too as a mother. When my daughters cry I want to do everything in my power to console them. Both for them, as it's truly awful witnessing their pain, but also for me, as their dysregulation dysregulates me! In that moment, when their suffering (or their shock or anger) is so intense that they scream at the top of their lungs, all I want them to do is, well . . . stop. *'Shhh, don't cry.'*

Learning Note: When in situations like the one I describe above, a really good way to respond to a person who is expressing themselves and their emotions through the healing power of tears is to sit with them or hold them, and allow them to freely express themselves in whatever way they feel compelled to. If you would like to offer words of affirmation, try, 'I'm here with you, cry for as long as you need to, let it all out.' This shows the person that you are there supporting them and that their distress is not too much for you to bear. I'm not perfect, so when it comes to my children, I don't always hit the mark. Often I'm tired or under pressure to get them out the door for school or to bed, but this way of being with them when they are upset is my goal, and one I try to meet as often as I can. You may not always feel resourced enough within yourself to show up for the other person in this way; however, it is a beautiful aim to hold in mind, and one we can do our best to strive for (while also being compassionate with ourselves when or if we don't quite get it right).

THE FUNCTION OF OUR EMOTIONS
Your emotions are your greatest teachers. Listen to them.
THIBAUT MEURISSE

Despite my mother doing a wonderful job of modelling my emotions to me as a little girl, I always found them extremely difficult to bear. I was a deeply sensitive soul who drank in everything that was happening around me: people's emotions, their body language and unsaid words, tension, aggression, conflict. It was like I possessed a sixth sense; I just had to look at someone to know how they were feeling. But, particularly at such an early age, I felt completely overwhelmed by this knowledge and so tried to detach from it, and indeed my own emotions, as best I could. I did this by bottling it all up inside me. Whatever happened, or whatever I experienced, I suppressed it. I would drink it all in, but once swallowed, I would hold it deep inside my body where it manifested as scary butterflies in my tummy or my head, circling with worry. Other people's emotions, as well as the deep spectrum of emotions I carried because of my own experiences in the world, weighed me down enormously and for much of my childhood I imagined myself as a rabbit caught in headlights, holding my breath in fear because I knew another emotion, whether mine or someone else's, would hit before I knew it. If only I had understood back then the importance of our emotions and that, if we can allow ourselves to listen to them, they are our greatest teachers and gift in life.

So much has changed since then because now, in my work as a psychologist, I have the privilege of witnessing emotions every single day, and I experience them as exactly that: a privilege to behold. Like back then, I see these emotions and feel them for the other person almost as intensely as they feel them for themselves. Not only that, but I often recognise them before the other person. This isn't surprising; this is my area of expertise and a craft I trained for many years to hone. However, what *was* extremely surprising for me during my first years as a psychologist was the lack of understanding people have about their emotions. This is mainly because most people are never taught this incredibly valuable information.

Let me show you what I mean:

REFLECTIVE EXERCISE

Reach for a pen and paper, and as best you can, spend a moment or two writing out the function (or purpose) of each of the following emotions:

Anger	Shame
Sadness	Joy
Fear	Happiness
Disgust	

Pause here to complete this exercise before continuing.

How did you do? Did you find it easy to complete our first reflective exercise? Or, like the vast majority of my clients, did this exercise cause you to pause and think, 'Hmm, I'm not actually sure of some (or all!) or these.' If you found it easy, well done! You can check your answers below as I outline the functions of these emotions in detail for you. If the latter, please don't worry, as (1) you very likely were never taught this information, and (2) you have arrived exactly where you were meant to in reaching for this book. I am going to teach you this and so much more over the coming steps.

So what are the functions of our emotions? Let's take a look.

ANGER

Where there is anger, there is always pain underneath.
ECKHART TOLLE

> *One of my most prominent memories of anger is deeply ingrained within me. I'm 13 and in my first year of secondary school. My three best friends are in my house for a sleepover and they've just wrestled my brand-new, much longed-for phone from my hands. I am pulsating with anger and so dysregulated that I am shouting uncontrollably at them, 'GIVE IT BACK, GIVE IT BACK', and banging on the locked door they are hiding behind. The reason I'm so emotionally fraught? They have just sent a text message to my crush and I am feeling extremely exposed and full to the brim with rage: 'How could they do this to me? My life is over!'*

According to the American Psychological Association, 'anger is a natural, adaptive response to threat; it inspires powerful, often aggressive, feelings and behaviours, which allow us to fight and to defend ourselves when we are attacked.' In the above example of anger, this definition rings wholly true. I am powerfully and aggressively attempting to defend myself from the threat my friends are imposing on me. I am doing everything in my power to overturn the situation I have found myself in and I won't back down until I have my phone safely back in my hands. My example may seem trivial to you, but even as I type these words I can feel remnants of that angry energy flowing through me. Why it stands out so viscerally in my mind, I'm not sure, but it does, and I know I will never forget the experience for as long as I live!

> *I also remember feeling intense anger on the day my parents told me who my birth mother was; someone very close to me whom I had known all my life. Another anger-related memory is from the aftermath of my father's death; I was furious that he had left me. (He had no choice in the matter, but anger isn't always rational!)*

I remember too a blazing row with my boyfriend (now my husband) many moons ago when he booked flights to Vegas on a whim without telling me until he was on the plane (he was brave!). A memory surfaces too of someone asking me when I planned to start exercising, just two weeks after the birth of my first baby, and in the same breath, when I was going to have another, because 'only children are so sensitive'. (I grew up as an only child, so you can imagine my reaction to this comment ... but maybe she had a point!)

I share these examples with you because anger can be triggered within us for many reasons, but it always plays a role. Our anger comes to protect us and to keep us safe. It is a message to us: 'This doesn't feel good; stand up for yourself.' It is a gift, a learning to us, a guidance. So often we berate ourselves for experiencing anger – 'I'm overreacting, I need to calm down' – but anger is a healthy and valid emotion that is so incredibly important for us to experience and listen to.

REFLECTIVE EXERCISE

Call to mind a time you felt incredibly angry. With a pen and paper, document the situation.

For example:

What sparked it?

How were you feeling in the moment, both emotionally and physically?

What thoughts were racing through your head?

How did you behave (or what did you do) when faced with your anger?

Did you learn anything from this experience?

Pause here to complete this exercise before continuing.

Take your time while doing so, and be gentle with yourself in the process. Dredging up memories such as these can be painful and extremely evocative, but trust yourself and trust the process. In honouring our emotions, we are honouring ourselves and letting go of so much of the weight we carry.

Other feelings that fall within the ANGER category:

Frustrated	Cross
Pissed off	Infuriated
Annoyed	Furious
Mad	In a rage

SADNESS

Every man has his secret sorrows which the world knows not; and often times we call a man cold when he is only sad.
HENRY WADSWORTH LONGFELLOW

My greatest pain and sadness in life was the death of my father. I will never forget the day a family friend arrived to his hospital bedside to give him the last rites. It was just myself, my mother and my unconscious father in the room, after the flow of visitors had quietened. My family had always felt small, as it was just the three of us, but only in that moment did the smallness hit home. Soon our trio would become a twosome. I sobbed my heart out on that day. It felt so real. So final. So imminent. In that hospital room my heart broke in two. I had always thought heartbreak was reserved for the ending of relationships with lovers, but on that day, in that lonely, dimly lit hospital room, I felt my heart shatter in a way it had never done before. Funnily enough, that day, in that hospital room, is the moment of sadness that most stands out to me in the loss of my father. Not the moment he took his last breath; not as the cover was placed on his coffin; and not in the church as we gathered to say goodbye; but in that hospital room as the priest prayed for my father's soul. As I sit here now reminiscing, it brings me right back to the pain. My heart feels heavy. My breath feels stuck and my eyes feel tired. These sensations are familiar, I experience them often, and each time they arrive they help me to release some of the sadness that my heart still holds (and will forever hold).

Sadness is an emotion that is strongly linked to loss. Loss can take many forms – the ending of a relationship or a particular situation, a feeling of rejection or disappointment, a big, or sometimes even small, life change or realisation, or through sickness or death. As with almost everything, sadness spans a spectrum, from the emotion you experience when you finish a book you really enjoyed to the intense pain you go through following losing a loved one. Like all our emotions, sadness has a function. It signals to us our need to care for and look after ourselves, and to others that we are in need of comfort and grace.

REFLECTIVE EXERCISE

Call to mind a time you felt deeply sad. With a pen and paper, document the situation. For example:

What brought on this sadness?

How were you feeling in the moment, both emotionally and physically in your body?

What thoughts were present in your mind?

How did you behave (or what did you do) while experiencing this sadness?

What did you need at that time in your life?

Did you learn anything from this deeply painful moment?

Pause here to complete this exercise before continuing.

Invite in the emotions that arrive as you do so, witnessing them and accepting them rather than trying to push them away as may be familiar to you. Allow yourself to feel them and to honour them, and in turn you will slowly begin to release them and their weight.

Often it is really easy for us to identify the needs of small children, for example when they are sad and clearly displaying this emotion. We are so used to meeting their needs, for example if they are hungry or tired, if their nappy needs changing or if they are seeking affection or love, but it is often far harder for us to pin point *our* needs, especially as typically we race through life juggling all of the responsibilities we carry and pushing our emotions aside.

REFLECTIVE PAUSE

When was the last time you considered your needs and how you could meet them for yourself?

Consider this question before reading on.

When I lost my father I needed many things. Comfort from loved ones. Time to feel and honour my emotions. Space to grieve and to care for myself following this huge loss in my life. Sleep – I was exhausted by the emotion of it all. Food to nourish and nurture my body as I navigated this journey. Understanding and patience, both from myself and from those around me.

Other feelings that fall within the SADNESS category:

Pain	Emptiness
Hurt	Low mood
Loss	Depression
Grief	A sense of helplessness or hopelessness

FEAR

Fear cuts deeper than swords.
GEORGE R.R. MARTIN

When I finished my doctorate in 2015 I went travelling in India. I had invested so many years into becoming a psychologist, and after all my hard work my dream had finally come true. This trip was a reward to myself after pouring my heart and soul into my training and coming out the other side (if slightly bruised and battered!).

My memories of India will always be some of my favourites. I went to Delhi, Rishikesh, Agra, Ranthambore, Jaipur, Mumbai and Goa, and fell in love with absolutely everything about the country. One memory that really stands out is an internal flight I took from Delhi to Rishikesh. I'll never forget walking out on the airport tarmac to see the tiny propeller plane that was transferring us to the Himalayas. It took my breath away. As I scrambled on board I reassured myself that all would be well, but the next 45 minutes were the scariest of my life. Never before have I witnessed turbulence like we experienced that day. It was so extreme that the overhead bins opened, raining their contents onto the passengers, and cans of beer and Coca-Cola on the food and beverage trolleys burst, showering us with spray. Everyone on the plane, even the air stewards, clung to their seats screaming, and despite not being particularly religious at the time, I prayed to God that I would not die. Thankfully my prayers were answered and we landed safely on Rishikesh soil. I spent the subsequent week in a yoga ashram eating vegetarian food and twisting and turning my body like I never had before, but, my oh my, how that fear stayed with me.

Interestingly, fear is the emotion that is discussed most frequently in my therapy room. Fear evolved to keep us safe and protect us from harm. When our brain perceives a threat, whether physical (like a speeding car), emotional (watching a scary movie), psychological (a fear of small spaces or heights), or imagined (catastrophising that our loved one is dead because they don't answer the phone), it sets off an alarm-triggering adaptive process in our body and brain that results in the 'fight, flight, freeze or fawn' stress response. When it comes to fear, many people also experience anxiety, which is a generalised response that is future-based and involves worrying about a threat that may or may not happen. With fear, the threat is known, present and definite, while with anxiety, the threat has not yet arrived and may never do so.

REFLECTIVE EXERCISE

Call to mind a time you felt immense fear. With a pen and paper, document the situation.

For example:

What sparked it?

How were you feeling in the moment, both emotionally and physically?

What thoughts were racing through your head?

How did you behave (or what did you do) when faced with this threat?

Did you learn anything from this experience?

Pause here to complete this exercise before continuing.

Both fear and anxiety can be hugely debilitating to experience and can take a long time to recover from, so I urge you to be kind to yourself while reflecting on previous fear or anxiety you've experienced or while working through any fear that may currently be present for you. As with sadness, we all have needs when it comes to feeling safe and secure in life and living without fear (as far as possible, since fear is adaptive and a very normal human emotion), and it is incredibly important to consider what these needs are and to honour them.

Other feelings that fall within the FEAR category:

Scared	Nervous
Threatened	On edge
Anxious	Frightened
Worried	Persecuted

DISGUST

Fear is danger to your body,
But disgust is danger to your soul.
DIANE ACKERMAN

Disgust arises as an aversion to something we perceive as 'offensive, vulgar or pathogenic'. We experience it via our senses: sight, smell, taste, touch or sound; through the ideas, actions or presentations of others; or in relation to lessons we are taught within our families, cultures and societies. The reason we experience disgust is to keep us safe from the 'offensive, vulgar or pathogenic' item we are faced with, and when we do indeed experience disgust we typically distance ourselves from whatever it is we have encountered. Interestingly, intimacy and love are factors that tend to lower our levels of disgust, something that you may find true for you if you consider the relationships you hold with those closest in your life (think sharing a bathroom with your other half, or changing a baby's nappy).

> *Many years ago I worked with a young man named Shane who, alongside other difficulties, had an intense disgust for the soles of shoes. Even thinking about what could potentially be on the underside of his footwear repulsed him and caused him great distress, so much so that he never wore his shoes in his home, and the thought of doing so filled him with terror. As you can imagine, he wanted visitors to remove their shoes before entering his home, and he did everything in his power to ensure this happened; but if someone did not take off their shoes, it would heighten his distress immeasurably and cause him to spiral into an intense panic and cleaning frenzy. When Shane pictured the soles of shoes, his imagination conjured up vulgar, pathogenic germs and contaminants, which he found almost too much to bear, so he did everything he could to keep himself 'safe' from these 'offensive, vulgar and disgusting toxins', even though this behaviour impacted his life hugely.*

REFLECTIVE EXERCISE

Call to mind a time you felt intense disgust. This exercise is for your eyes only, so be honest! With a pen and paper, document the situation.

For example:

What sparked it?

How were you feeling in the moment, both emotionally and physically?

What thoughts were racing through your head?

How did you behave (or what did you do) when faced with your disgust?

Pause here to complete this exercise before continuing.

Pay attention to how completing this exercise feels for you. Do other emotions arrive with the disgust you are remembering? Perhaps you may even be judging yourself because of the experience you are calling to mind. Whatever is happening for you, be gentle with yourself and allow whatever unfolds for you. This is the work. This is the process. This is where healing comes.

Other feelings that fall within the DISGUST category:

Repelled	Horrified
Disapproving	Sickened
Appalled	Nauseated
Revolted	Stomach-turning

SHAME

Shame is the intensely painful feeling or experience of believing that we are flawed and therefore unworthy of love and belonging.
BRENÉ BROWN

Shame is the uncomfortable feeling in the pit of your stomach when you experience (or perceive to experience) other people's judgement. It's the rabbit-caught-in-headlights wild-eyed discomfort when you meet (or perceive to meet) others' disappointment. Shame is the 'I am wrong' (as opposed to 'I did wrong') sensation that burns through you, leaving you fearing rejection, isolation and ostracism. According to the American Psychological Association, shame is 'a highly unpleasant self-conscious emotion arising from the sense of there being something dishonourable, immodest, or indecorous in one's own conduct or circumstances'. While another person or circumstance can evoke shame within us, so too can an internal sense of wrongness or a sense of failure in meeting the standards, morals and values that we set ourselves.

Shame should not be confused with guilt, which is a sense that we have 'done wrong' and so want to make amends for our behaviours or shortcomings (more on this later!). It is the 'I am wrong or worthless' emotion we tend to hide or conceal and that we avoid discussing openly due to a sense of humiliation and deeply ingrained feelings of being flawed. The function of shame is to help us conform to societal and cultural rules and norms, which in turn helps us to engage in behaviours that benefit our communities and lead to us being accepted and valued by others and feeling a sense of belonging. Humans are social beings, and shame helps us to remain close to those around us and discourages us from engaging in behaviours that might jeopardise our standing in our communities, both big and small.

REFLECTIVE PAUSE

Can you think of someone who was ostracised in some way from either a small or very large community you were involved in?

Pause here to consider this before reading on.

In my very first year as a psychologist in training I worked with the most special soul, Julie, who was in her mid-twenties and had a three-year-old daughter named Lucy who was the centre of her world. She had just come out of an incredibly abusive relationship with Lucy's father. For seven years Julie remained trapped in a relationship with this man who abused her both physically and mentally in every way imaginable. For me, as I sat witnessing her pain week on week and the hugely traumatic impact this man had on her, the saddest part was that Julie carried such shame from this period of her life. After years of being told she was flawed, inadequate and worthless, she had internalised these beliefs, and although no one in the world ever deserves to be kicked and beaten and controlled at the hands of another, because of the vitriol this man rained on her, there was a part of Julie that felt she was responsible for the way she was treated. 'Why didn't I leave? I deserved to be abused given I stayed for so long.' 'How weak am I that I let him treat me that way for so long?' 'I am such a failure of a mother for staying in that house with him and allowing my child to witness what he did.'

Julie and I worked together for a number of months, and during this time, when Julie felt safe and ready to do so, we completed incredibly powerful chair work where Julie imagined this man sitting beside her in an empty chair and was able to speak to him in ways she had never before voiced. Julie found such freedom in this work and it allowed her to process and release many of the pent-up emotions she had been carrying for years, including the ferocious rage that was burning inside her. On the day Julie and I parted ways she gave me the most beautiful gift, one that will always be one of the highlights of my career: her parting words. She said, 'I no longer carry the shame I once did, and I know now, after all these years, that what happened to me wasn't my fault.' These words will stay in my heart forever, as I hope they do for Julie.

REFLECTIVE EXERCISE

Call to mind a time you felt intense shame. This exercise is for your eyes only, so engage with it as honestly as you can. With a pen and paper, document the situation and the associated emotions and feelings.

For example:

What sparked this sense of shame?

How were you feeling in the moment, both emotionally and physically?

What thoughts were racing through your head?

How did you behave (or what did you do) when you felt this way?

Were you able to let go of this shame or is it something you still carry?

Pause here to complete this exercise before continuing.

Offer yourself the same kindness and compassion you would a friend if they were brave enough to share a story such as yours with you. Remember you are only human, so please don't berate yourself for the human emotions you experience.

Other feelings that fall within the SHAME category:

Mortified	Abashed
Humiliated	Remorseful
Regretful	Contrite
Embarrassed	

HAPPINESS AND JOY

Joy does not simply happen to us.
We have to choose joy and keep choosing it every day.
HENRI J.M. NOUWEN

When I think of the happiest and most joy-filled moments of my life, many come to mind. There are the momentous occasions, like graduating from university with my parents by my side; my wedding day; the birth of my three beautiful daughters; the launch of my podcast and it hitting number one in the charts. My honeymoon also comes to mind, as do many other travel memories. Scuba diving in Thailand, watching the sunrise in Mexico, golden hour cocktails in Santorini, eating pasta and pizza in Rome. More intimate occasions come to mind too. My children's first steps. Celebrating my husband's promotion with champagne. Blowing out candles on a birthday cake in the middle of the Covid years. Getting our dog when he was just a tiny puppy. A carefree girls' weekend with friends I've known all my life. Simple pleasures also come to mind. Putting my feet up at the end of the day after ticking something challenging off my To Do list. An ice cream in the park on a hot summer's day. A sea swim, and a mug of cacao while wrapped in a warm towel. A hug. A meaningful compliment. An 'I love you'.

Happiness and joy are two related but distinct emotions. Happiness is an outward expression of emotion that is more fleeting and often sparked by exhilaration or excitement, while joy is an internal feeling and one that is longer-lasting. Joy is linked to meaning and purpose and is, according to the

American Psychological Association, 'a feeling of extreme gladness, delight, or exultation of the spirit arising from a sense of well-being or satisfaction'. To give you an example of the distinction, just this morning my daughter experienced pure and utter joy when she was reunited with her best friend from Montessori after a two-week holiday; and extreme happiness when she found an uneaten sweet in the pocket of her coat! Similarly, I felt so happy to have an extra hour in bed this morning while my husband got up with the girls, and utter joy when they came running in to say hello and to hug me after a hard day of work in school and Montessori.

The function of happiness and joy, like all our emotions, is to guide us. When that happiness- or joy-filled 'high' is sparked in our bodies it signals to us the things we enjoy in life and what feels meaningful, worthwhile and pleasurable. Happiness and joy also show us *who* leads us to feel content, at peace and grateful, and so we often choose to spend more time with these people, and less with those who cause us to feel otherwise. Research shows too that our joy and happiness levels (although controlled by up to 50 per cent by our genetics) are hugely impacted (by up to 40 per cent) by our habits and choices in life, while only a small amount (up to 10 per cent) of our happiness and joy levels are dictated by the circumstances we find ourselves in. Interesting statistics, aren't they? Ones that, without doubt, made me stop to think upon first reading them and I share them with you to encourage you to 'choose joy and keep choosing it every day', as this is how your happiness and joy levels will soar.

REFLECTIVE PAUSE

Call to mind a time you felt (1) extreme happiness and (2) utter joy.

Consider the beauty of these situations and what sparked the emotions you were experiencing at the time. Notice how your body responds as you allow yourself to sink in to these memories, perhaps you may even re-experience some of the beauty of the moment.

Pause here to consider this before reading on.

REFLECTIVE EXERCISE

Open your diary or the calendar on your phone and schedule the following joy moments across the next month:

1. One small joy moment per day to boost you, no matter what day of the week it is. Examples may exclude a protected 20 minutes to enjoy a mug of coffee, tea or cacao outside in the sunshine with no distractions, or, if you're anything like me, some chocolate in the evening when all the day's tasks are complete.

2. One (slightly bigger!) joy moment per week that's just for you. This could be dinner or coffee with a friend. A sea swim. A visit to the cinema or a sound bath. Think of something that feels like a real treat that you might not otherwise experience this week.

3. Look across the four weeks ahead and schedule in one (even bigger!) thing for yourself. Maybe afternoon tea or a day retreat. It could be a dinner date in a restaurant you've wanted to go to for ages, or a hike somewhere beautiful that you can schedule and really look forward to.

As you schedule in these events, reap the joy and happiness that comes flooding through you, as research has found that the anticipation of events can fill us with almost the same level of joy and happiness as the event itself. And don't forget to make a note in your diary for next month (and the one after that, and the one after that ...) to schedule in further joy moments (one per day, a slightly bigger one per week and an even bigger one per month). Perhaps this scheduling (and following through!) can be a new gift to yourself.

Pause here to complete this exercise before continuing.

Other feelings that fall within the HAPPINESS and JOY categories:

Grateful	Merry
Optimistic	Cheerful
Loving	Delighted
Gleeful	Jolly

SUPPRESSING OUR EMOTIONS VERSUS HONOURING THEM

Don't shoot the messengers
they are gardeners
bringing tears to water
the seeds of a new you.
VALENTINA QUARTA

So often we hide from our emotions. We numb them, dull them, dispel them ... or at least we *try* to. You see, the thing about emotions is that we can't numb them forever. The more we run from them, the more they bottle up inside us, placing immense pressure on our bodies. When we store our emotions within us our chest can feel tight, our head can pound, our shoulders can tense and our stomach can feel sick. We can also experience deep pain in our body from this experience, and sometimes, when we suppress our emotions for a really long time or if the emotions are incredibly painful or traumatic, they can manifest as disorders in our body.

REFLECTIVE PAUSE

Have you ever, seemingly out of nowhere, suddenly become flooded by emotion? Perhaps you're watching TV and a sad scene or an evocative song causes you to begin crying uncontrollably. Or perhaps you are with a loved one, going about your day, when you break into a rant without even knowing where it came from or what is going on. Often these moments surprise us, 'Why did I react like that? It came out of nowhere,' but in reality the emotion was suppressed within you, awaiting a release.

Pause here to consider this before reading on.

As a human being who experiences emotions every single day, I can relate, and I can think of many times when I've suppressed my emotions, especially as a child. Emotions that have overwhelmed me or scared me or have felt too painful for me to process. Emotions that I 'didn't have time for' or that I tried to pretend weren't really there. Emotions that felt like an inconvenience or that I believed I wasn't equipped to deal with. Even after becoming a psychologist and knowing about the importance of honouring our emotions!

Suppressing our emotions is something we all do, for many reasons. Perhaps it's how we were taught to deal with our emotions as we were growing up (whether explicitly, due to messages we received from our parents and caregivers, or implicitly, through watching them navigate their own emotions), or maybe we never learned how to navigate our emotions in a healthy and helpful way. Perhaps our emotions felt overwhelming and scary, too overwhelming and scary to face. In fact, this process can often be a coping or defence mechanism; we shut down our emotions to protect ourselves from them as we feel too vulnerable or in too much pain to deal with them.

We also often label our emotions 'good' or 'bad', 'positive' or negative', categorising them and picking and choosing the emotions we allow ourselves to feel. However, if we numb the 'bad', we also numb the 'good', and isn't that so sad? That we may be dulling our joy and happiness? *All* our emotions are signals sent to guide us. They are a gift, and one we should welcome with open arms because they offer us such valuable information. For example, they help us to understand how the people around us make us feel. Do we feel safe and content in their company and in how they interact with us? Are we happy when we're around them and do they leave us feeling better than when we met them? Conversely, I'm sure there has been a time in your life where you've felt irritated by how someone has spoken to you or treated you. What were your emotions signalling to you in this moment? Did you give yourself the gift of considering this? Our emotions also guide us on what matters to us and what's important in our lives. They help us to live a life that's true and authentic to us and that feels meaningful. Isn't that gorgeous? And isn't that something you wish for yourself? I know it is how I would like to live my one and precious life.

REFLECTIVE PAUSE

What is your relationship with your emotions like? Do you allow yourself to feel them or do you push them down, numbing and dulling them? If the latter, why do you think you do this? Does this tactic work or do they escape to the surface regardless, often when you least expect them or want them to?

Spend a moment considering these questions before moving on. If you would like to really reflect on these questions, reach for a piece of paper and a pen and write down the thoughts that come. Take your time. There is no need to rush this process, so give yourself this gift and reap the rewards that will come.

If you can relate to any (or all) of the above, you are not alone, I promise you. In fact, so often I see people suppressing their emotions in my therapy room, or categorising them as good and bad, and as I shared above, this is something I too do when my emotions feel too much for me, as they sometimes do for us all. But no matter what your relationship has been like with your emotions up to now, you have found yourself here at this very moment for a reason, and with my help, it's time to begin honouring your emotions and working through them so that you can reach a place of freedom within your mind, body and soul.

LEARNING TO HONOUR YOUR EMOTIONS

Instead of resisting emotion, the best way to dispel it is to enter it fully, embrace it and see through your resistance.
DEEPAK CHOPRA

When we have been suppressing our emotions for a long time, it can feel really scary to decide to open our hearts to them. It can also feel like something we have no idea how to do. This is where I come in, and the power of immersing yourself fully in this book. So place your hand on your heart and thank yourself for beginning this journey, for it has led you here and handed you the key to truly transform your life.

To make this journey as easy as possible for you I have created steps to guide you through the process. Take your time with these steps and be gentle with yourself as you journey through them. Allow yourself the gift of time and space. There's no rush. After relating to your emotions in the way you have all these years, learning to navigate them in a new way may feel unfamiliar and even a little daunting, so go gently.

1. CREATE SPACE AND TIME FOR YOUR EMOTIONS

When it comes to honouring your emotions, something that is really important is to create space and time to allow yourself to feel them and to work through them so you can come to a place of release, and in turn, inner peace. For this reason, I encourage you to carve out time in your day to do this work and to do so in a space that feels comfortable, safe and, if possible, is distraction-free. Think snuggling up somewhere cosy with a blanket and perhaps even lighting some candles or playing some soft soothing music. Or, if your emotions arise out of nowhere, as they often do, consider how and where you can find a space to safely feel them in the moment. This may be retreating to a safe space in your house, or your office in work. You may decide to take five minutes to sit in the safety of your car or to walk to your favourite park and sit in a quiet corner where you will have privacy. The idea is to carve out time to prioritise feeling your emotions, and to do so in a space that will facilitate this process for you.

Note: If you have been suppressing your emotions for a significant time, or if the emotions you are carrying inside you are deeply painful or traumatic, perhaps the safe space to connect with them is the therapy room with someone you feel comfortable and at ease with. Often people share with me that they feel undeserving of taking up a space like this, but if you are struggling, or if facing into this process feels particularly daunting for you, I urge you to seek support to help you navigate this journey.

2. SIT WITH YOUR EMOTIONS TO FEEL AND UNDERSTAND THEM

We often hear the term 'sit with your emotions', but what does it actually mean? How do we actually do it? The answer is very simple: when an emotion is present for you, allow yourself to connect with it and spend time with it in a gentle and welcoming way. Here's how:

- To begin, lean in to the feelings you are experiencing in your body. What do they feel like physiologically and where are you feeling them within you? Does your body feel tense or heavy or are you experiencing any sensations in particular parts of your body? However you are feeling, what is it like to be engaging in this process and experiencing these sensations? Spend time connecting with yourself in this way with an open and curious mind and with patience.

- Next, as best you can, and without judgement, pay attention to the thoughts that are accompanying this experience. What thoughts are arriving for you in this moment? Are they familiar or new? Are they fast and overwhelming or are they slow and painful? What tone are they taking and how are they making you feel as you witness them? Perhaps you would like to put pen to paper to help you process and keep track of these thoughts or to explore if more will come to you through welcoming them in this way. Writing helps me hugely when I'm unsure of how I am feeling and often the words that arrive on the page surprise me but make perfect sense. Allow yourself the time you need with this process; this is the work, this is the healing and you have the power within you to meet yourself here in this way.

- A really important part of this process is to identify the emotions and feelings you are experiencing, and, if you can, *why* they are showing up for you. It may be that when your emotion arrives you have no idea what you are experiencing or the reason why you are feeling this way, but if you sit with these physical sensations and accompanying thoughts, you will be in a much better position to identify these answers. To help with this process, look at the Feelings Wheel on page 35. Spend some time sitting with this to familiarise yourself with it; or, when you experience a particular emotion that has arrived, use this picture to guide and support you.

3. RELEASE YOUR EMOTIONS

All our emotions carry an energetic charge. Think about it: when you are deeply upset or bursting with happiness, or so angry that you feel an intense rage, you experience an energetic sensation in your body, right? It is this energetic charge or emotional energy that, when released, benefits us hugely. It's like a saucepan boiling on the hob; we lower the temperature or remove the lid to release pressure. This is exactly what we are aiming for when we want to release emotional energy from our body. If we don't release this energetic charge, we store it, and feel it in our bodies, or it erupts when we least expect or want it to.

There are many ways in which we can release emotional energy. The choice is yours.

- You may find talking to a loved one or mental health professional particularly helpful; or, like me, you may feel drawn to expressing and releasing it through writing it down and getting it off your chest.

- Similarly, you may experience a deeply healing release through allowing tears to fall and cleanse you, or you may experience a huge sense of relief by using a cushion as a punchbag or by repeatedly throwing it across the room, or by holding it against your face as you scream into it.

- Moving your body is another really healthy way to release emotional charge. A brisk walk or a run may help you to feel lighter and freer, or you could turn to somatic techniques to shake the energy out of your body. Likewise you could brush down the energy by rubbing your hands down your torso, arms and legs; or, to soothe and support yourself as you allow your emotions to naturally release, engage in butterfly taps or a gentle affirming hug (see Step Three for a step-by-step account of how to complete these exercises).

- Dancing as if no one is watching is another great way to complete this work, or you could use gentle stretches or yoga poses to slowly and deeply feel this desired release.

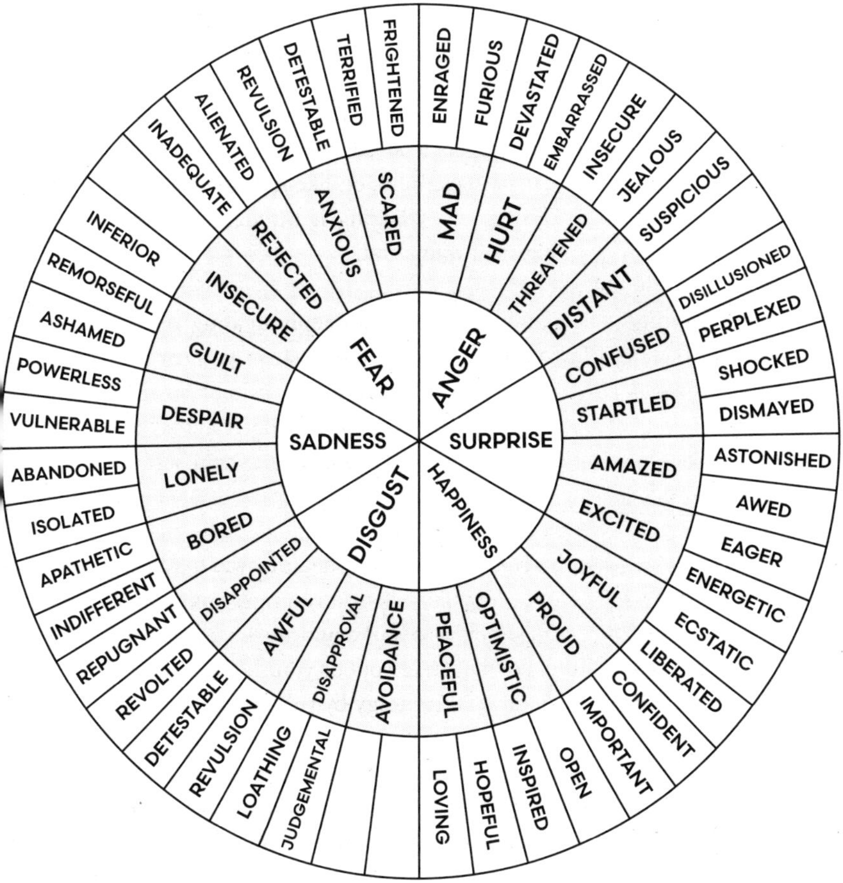
ANGER
SURPRISE
HAPPINESS
DISGUST
SADNESS
FEAR
MAD
HURT
THREATENED
DISTANT
CONFUSED
STARTLED
AMAZED
EXCITED
JOYFUL
PROUD
OPTIMISTIC
PEACEFUL
AVOIDANCE
DISAPPROVAL
AWFUL
DISAPPOINTED
BORED
LONELY
DESPAIR
GUILT
INSECURE
REJECTED
ANXIOUS
SCARED
ENRAGED
FURIOUS
DEVASTATED
EMBARRASSED
INSECURE
JEALOUS
SUSPICIOUS
DISILLUSIONED
PERPLEXED
SHOCKED
DISMAYED
ASTONISHED
AWED
EAGER
ENERGETIC
ECSTATIC
LIBERATED
CONFIDENT
IMPORTANT
OPEN
INSPIRED
HOPEFUL
LOVING
JUDGEMENTAL
LOATHING
REVULSION
DETESTABLE
REVOLTED
REPUGNANT
INDIFFERENT
APATHETIC
ISOLATED
ABANDONED
VULNERABLE
POWERLESS
ASHAMED
REMORSEFUL
INFERIOR
INADEQUATE
ALIENATED
REVULSION
DETESTABLE
TERRIFIED
FRIGHTENED

- Likewise, expressing yourself through writing about, drawing or painting how you are feeling can be deeply healing and can lead to a beautiful release of the emotional charge you have been carrying.

REFLECTIVE EXERCISE

Choose one of the following exercises to complete (or all of them if you feel compelled to engage in this exercise as deeply as possible). Do so at a time that feels convenient and safe, in a space that, if possible, is distraction-free. Be gentle with yourself as you complete this exercise. Take your time and allow whatever emotions arrive to do so. There is no right or wrong here, only learning and release, both of which will bring you one step closer to inner peace.

a) Call to mind a moment in time when you felt deeply emotional. This may be a situation or emotion that you are currently carrying, or it may be one from the past. To benefit most from this exercise it is important to choose a scenario that will conjure up emotion for you, but not so much emotion that it feels too much for you to bear. Once you have called this emotion to mind: On a piece of paper or in your journal write down everything that comes to you. Write down all your thoughts, all your pain, all the heaviness you have been carrying. Allow yourself to write freely; let the words come, with no agenda or pressure. This exercise is one to help you lighten the burden you have been carrying and the pain you have been experiencing. This is freeing, this is healing, this is the work.

Or:

b) Move your body in a way you feel called to, to release the emotional energy you are experiencing and carrying.

You may decide to go for a walk or a run, to stretch or to practise yoga, to dance as if no one is watching or to gently soothe your body through somatic techniques. However you choose to move your body is up to you. Do so lovingly, and enjoy the release and peace this exercise brings.

Or:

c) Plan a moment of connection with a loved one and share with them how you have been feeling recently. Allow yourself to truly open up to them and to share your vulnerability. Show up as your true authentic self and as a normal human being who experiences painful emotions and struggles, just as we all do. Allow yourself to be supported by this person and to welcome in their love and care.

Note: If you decide to complete option (c), spend a moment considering who the right person is for you to connect with in this way. From previous experience, we will typically have a sense of who will be able to meet us and support us in our vulnerability, and who may not have the capacity to do so in a way we are yearning for. So choose wisely; and if a loved one doesn't automatically come to mind, consider the services available to you, a list of which you will find in the appendix of this book.

4. ASK YOURSELF WHAT YOU NEED IN THIS MOMENT

Doing this work can be incredibly hard and deeply painful, so as you are sitting with your emotions in this new way and processing how you are feeling, ask yourself what you need in this moment to support and nurture you as you navigate this journey. Some examples might be: a cup of tea and some time out before returning to reality; a hug from a loved one; soothing and comforting your body using somatic techniques; some fresh air; being gentle with yourself for the rest of the day and allowing yourself to do the easier tasks on your To Do list and to leave the heavy lifting until tomorrow; a bath and an early night.

Only you will know what your needs are, so pause to consider what it is that you are yearning for and listen to the whispers of your heart.

STEP ONE HONOUR YOUR EMOTIONS SUMMARY

Our emotions are gifts sent to guide us. No matter what the situation or circumstance, our emotions are always with us, signalling how we are feeling and what we need in each moment. My emotions have never let me down. Even when they have erupted so suddenly that they have caught me off guard and I have done or said something that afterwards I deeply regretted, I am always thankful for my emotions because they highlight my areas of pain and the parts of myself that I need to gently heal and pay attention to. Our emotions offer us valuable lessons and guidance that will eventually set us free, as it is only when we heal these hidden parts of ourselves that we truly experience inner peace.

As we come to the end of Step One Honour Your Emotions it is important to acknowledge that sitting with our emotions can be incredibly painful. This work is hard, so it makes sense that we often try to run from our emotions or push them down deep inside of us, but doing so can cause us to feel a deep sense of heaviness, and this suppressed emotional energy will continue to put pressure on us for as long as we bury it. However, now, with the practices and processes you have learned throughout Step One, you are equipped to sit with your emotions, feel them and release them in a safe and gentle way, while also looking after yourself. This is the work; and it is work that is deeply transformative. By joining me on this journey you now have the power to not only honour your emotions, but to honour yourself, and to heal and release the pain you have been carrying inside you for far too long. Be brave and be bold, and give yourself the gift of setting yourself free. I wish you luck on your journey to honour your emotions; and, remember, no emotion is permanent – they fluctuate and float like the wind.

STEP TWO

CALM THE CHAOS OF YOUR MIND

*The mind is like water.
When it's turbulent,
it's difficult to see.
When it's calm,
everything becomes clear.*
PRASAD MAHES

If there's been one constant in my life, it's been anxiety. Always present. Always influencing my decisions. Always a part of me. I think back now to my early childhood and I can feel it in my body. The clenching gut. The uncertainty in my mind. The tension in my shoulders. 'Will my friends always want to be my friend?'; 'When is Mum coming to collect me? I'm tired and I just want to feel safe'; 'I feel so uncomfortable in such a large group. I don't know what to say or do or how to act.'

It wasn't until my late teens that I could name it. I always thought it was just me. A part of me. My personality and temperament and way of being in the world all wrapped up in one. The shy little girl who stayed quiet in large groups but who eventually came into her own when one-on-one with her friends after the excitement had died down. The happy but reserved teen who carefully watched on as life happened around her, assessing who and what felt safe and inviting. Even now, the adult whose bodily sensations guide so much of my decisions and my feelings of safety as I navigate the world.

It saddens me to realise this. I wish life could have felt more carefree, more easy, more natural. Instead I was always on the lookout, one eye open for threat. A threat that was constantly there. A threat that my inner child still carries, even after all these years and the countless books I've read and hours I've sat in the therapy chair. Of course I understand it now. I get it. Why I was always so scared, why she (my inner child) was always so scared. But that doesn't make it any less sad. I live far more peacefully now, having learned techniques to soothe it and keep my anxiety at bay, but it will always be a part of me ... just one that no longer has the same hold on me as it once had.

I imagine many of you reading this can relate. The constant fear. The feeling on edge. The exhaustion that comes hand in hand with living in threat mode. Countless hours I sat in GPs' offices proclaiming how exhausted I was. 'Are you exercising?', 'Yes'. 'Are you drinking water?', 'Yes'. 'Are you sleeping?', 'Yes'. But it was always mental exhaustion. It was the hypervigilance and cortisol circling through my body. It was the anxiety.

So often people in my therapy room tell me that they've always been 'a worrier'. 'So you've always suffered from anxiety?' I gently reply. They pause, struck by what I've just said and then utter a quiet 'Yes. I never thought about it that way. I just thought it was a part of me. My personality and temperament and way of being in the world all wrapped up in one.' I smile because I get it. More than they know. I get the impact this has had on their life. The bone-shattering tiredness. The intense fear. The never feeling safe.

Not just that, but I get the impact anxiety has had on *your* life.

If you can indeed relate to my words, to my story, what can you do? Does life always have to feel this hard? No. Your anxiety might always be a part of your life, but you can quieten it. You can soothe it. You can understand it and work with it and honour it so that it no longer has such a tight hold over you.

When my anxiety arises now it is usually because my inner child is scared. Something is happening in my life that is causing her to sit up and say, 'This doesn't feel safe. This reminds me of a hurt I once experienced and I'll do anything I can to avoid feeling that pain again.' So now, when she becomes activated, I listen to her and reassure her: 'You are safe. There is nothing to fear. We aren't in danger and I am with you.' I also draw on CBT techniques such as challenging my anxious thoughts to assess whether they are true and valid, and if they're not (as they typically aren't), I rationalise how I am feeling, which brings me calm. I also breathe and practise somatic techniques. I take slow and deep breaths in and out to calm my nervous system and show my body that there is no threat, except the one in my mind.

The good news is that all these strategies work. Anxiety might always be a part of me, but it's one I can manage now, and one *you* can learn to manage too.

THE WHATS AND WHYS OF ANXIETY

Worrying does not take away tomorrow's troubles,
it takes away today's peace.
RANDY ARMSTRONG

Before I guide you through the incredibly powerful ways you can learn to control your anxiety so it no longer controls you (and, in turn, change your life; something I do not say lightly), let's first look at what anxiety actually is and the science behind it. Believe it or not, anxiety is actually a natural bodily reaction and something we are *all* evolutionarily primed to experience to keep us safe from harm.

You see, when our body thinks we are at risk of harm it sends a signal to our brain: DANGER. This signal swiftly activates our fight, flight, freeze or fawn response. Imagine being in a cage with a bear. To protect us, our body prepares us to fight the bear; flee, or run from the bear; freeze in front of the bear; or fawn, try to placate the bear. When our brain perceives an imminent threat, whether real, such as an oncoming car, or imagined, such as catastrophising someone is dead because they aren't answering their phone – we've all been there! – adrenaline is released in our brain to send a signal to our body that we are in imminent danger. This brings about a physiological response. Our heart begins to beat faster, pumping blood to our organs. Our breathing increases. Our muscles tense. Our senses are heightened. During this process our brain releases cortisol to curb bodily functions that are non-essential in dangerous situations and to fuel our body's response to the danger. This is our body's way of preparing us to keep ourselves safe, as best we can, and I have no doubt it sounds familiar to you. The racing heart, the clenched fists and tense shoulders, the flush of heat that occurs when our body is furiously pumping blood to our organs, the butterflies in our tummy due to all of the hormones and chemicals flooding our body.

However, here's the difficulty when it comes to anxiety sufferers like you and me. Our body reacts to both real or imagined threats in exactly the same way because, unfortunately, our brain cannot tell the difference, so – in very simple terms – this is what leads us to experience anxiety. Because of this, many of us find it extremely difficult to control our anxiety, which can lead to our anxiety symptoms being persistent, debilitating and hugely impactful on our lives.

STRESS AND OVERWHELM

It's not the load that breaks you, it's the way you carry it.
LOU HOLTZ

The same can be said about stress and this too is a process our body is primed to experience. Mental and emotional stress occurs when we are faced with more demands than we believe we are resourced to handle, and this is where the overwhelm sets in and we feel as if we can't cope with everything we are carrying on our shoulders.

We've all been there. It's exam year in school and we are juggling multiple subjects, aural and oral examinations, and practical tasks *go leor*. It's extremely overwhelming, especially coupled with the pressure to succeed so we can navigate a career that will serve us for the rest of our lives.

Or maybe it's a first date with someone you really like. You are doing everything in your power to dress in a way that you think the other person will find attractive and to portray yourself in the best possible light as someone who is funny, caring, intelligent and worthy of a second date.

Perhaps you're working on a once-in-a-lifetime project in your career or going for a promotion that you really want and so you set yourself the mammoth task of achieving the impossible over the next week so you can shine as brightly as possible and achieve all the goals that you carry in your heart.

There's a possibility, too, that, like me, you're a parent juggling a hundred and one balls, none of which you feel you can set down, so your hands keep spinning and you continue ticking off all the To Dos you feel you have to achieve within the limited time frame available to you, all the while working on far less sleep than you need.

Just as the function of anxiety is to keep us safe, stress also serves a function in our lives; it motivates us to perform and to achieve. But it can also send us a warning sign when we are feeling over-stretched and burdened beyond capacity. As we saw in Step One Honour Your Emotions, when I presented our emotions as a gift that come to guide us, stress can also be a gift. It can make us pause and evaluate all we are carrying, the impact this weight is having on us, and how we might begin to set down some of the balls we are juggling so that we can slow down, take a deep breath and make life feel more manageable for ourselves and for our health.

When it comes to stress, and indeed anxiety, it is our relationship with these difficulties that is paramount in how we respond to them and manage them. As Lou Holtz said, 'it's not the load that breaks you, it's the way you carry it' and this is very true in relation to these experiences we are biologically primed to feel. If we can learn to recognise *when* we are experiencing stress and anxiety, which both incur the same biological process within us (fight, flight, freeze or fawn), and *why* our bodies are reacting in this way, we can take control of the system at play and calm and soothe it.

So how do we do this?

REFLECTIVE EXERCISE

Grab your journal or a piece of paper, and write a letter outlining your anxiety or stress journey across your lifetime. You can address this letter to your anxiety or stress if this feels right for you, or, more simply, to yourself.

In your letter document aspects of your stress and anxiety, for example:

Where and when you first remember experiencing this difficulty

How it made you feel, both physically and emotionally

Factors that trigger this difficulty in your life

Things that made/make it worse

Things that made/make it better

Where you are now with this difficulty in your life

What this journey has taught you

Take as long as you need to craft this letter and do so in a space that feels safe and comfortable. This is the work, this is where the magic happens, this is where you begin to transform your life.

CALMING THE CHAOS OF OUR MINDS
Set peace of mind as your highest goal and organise your life around it.
BRIAN TRACY

In the almost 20 years I have been immersed in the world of psychology, both as a trainee psychologist (doing all I could to perfect my craft), and, as a qualified psychologist (who as the years progressed realised I would never perfect my craft!), and indeed as a client sitting in the opposite chair, doing the work, searching for inner peace, witnessing the healing, my understanding of how to meaningfully calm the chaos of our minds has grown. Anxiety and stress (and the associated overwhelm) are difficulties clients bring to my therapy room every day and, for this reason, are areas I research and work with constantly. The world of psychology has introduced me to many wonderful ways to soothe psychological and emotional distress, and I often turn to these techniques both in the therapy room and when I feel that my own alarm signals are activated. However, the work I believe heals most deeply the 'chaos of the mind' and the huge fear I so often see in my clients' eyes, is threefold:

1. Having a safe space to process the original wounds that have led to this distress (for example, in my case, my adoption experience) in the presence of a non-judgemental, compassionate and trusted other.

2. Healing the scared inner child who lies deep within every single one of us, and who can feel such immense fear and overwhelm because of all they have witnessed in life; and the part of them that is doing all they can to protect us from experiencing this pain again.

3. Regulating our nervous system and lowering the stress hormones that our body releases when it feels we are in danger or under threat. So often, we are living in 'fight, flight, freeze or fawn' mode without even realising it because we are living such busy, hectic lives and juggling so many balls. Regulating our nervous system is a skill that can be taught and it will bring us from 'fight, flight, freeze or fawn' back into 'rest and digest' mode, where we feel safe and our body feels able to relax and rest. This is so important for our health in so many ways.

Step Three is all about regulating your nervous system, but before we move on to that, let's look at these other two processes individually:

ENGAGING IN THERAPY

Therapy is a gift. It is a chance to finally be heard, understood and supported.
BESSEL VAN DER KOLK

Engaging in therapy has been one of the greatest gifts of my life. My first introduction to the process was when, as a sullen seventeen-year-old who had just found out that, unbeknownst to me, I had known my biological mother all my life, my parents arranged for a therapist to visit our house. I will always remember sitting on our sofa that day sandwiched between my anxious parents and refusing to speak. I was so angry at my parents for keeping this huge secret from me (something that had been advised to them by adoption professionals when I joined their family as a newborn baby) and not ready to process this anger or to speak about it. Looking back, refusing to speak may have been a way for me to take control of something when everything else was falling apart around me, but this certainly wasn't a conscious decision at the time.

My next foray with therapy was during my undergraduate psychology degree. I was finding it hard to navigate my relationship with my biological family at the time (as is so common for adopted people, due to the complexity of the situation), so I sought support from a local therapist, Marie. Marie was a no-nonsense woman in her late 40s who welcomed me into her therapy room in an incredibly warm and caring way. It was Marie who introduced me to inner child work, something that years later drastically changed my approach and understanding of therapy as a psychologist. I found my sessions with Marie incredibly powerful and began to understand myself for the first time in my life. In our transference (a process that occurs in therapy where the client projects their feelings about someone else in their life onto the therapist) Marie represented the biological mother who never nurtured or cared for me, and she supported me wholly and completely throughout the work we engaged in together. Marie's therapy room was a sanctuary for me and with her help, I opened up in ways I had never done before. Marie was non-judgemental and validating throughout our work together and our beautiful relationship allowed me to reveal my true authentic self and my deepest thoughts, feelings and desires, something that was deeply healing.

Since my journey with Marie, I have time and again witnessed the truly beautiful and deeply healing, transformative power of therapy, and when it comes to soothing the distress of anxiety and stress, and indeed the chaos of our minds, therapy is without doubt a modality that I recommend and encourage others to engage in. Having a therapist by your side to support you as you navigate a journey of self-discovery is like nothing else and the experience can only be believed by someone who has engaged in the process, but, most importantly, with the right person.

Have you been yearning to step into this process?

INNER CHILD HEALING

The wounded inner child is our bringer of healing … one who makes whole.
CARL JUNG

Inner child work is one of the most powerful healing modalities I have ever experienced in the therapy room, particularly for soothing anxiety and stress and calming the chaos of our minds. For countless years I've been mesmerised as clients soothe intense anxiety, pain and distress through connecting inwards and offering their inner child what he or she is most yearning for. This may be love, comfort, gentle soothing, or simply no longer feeling alone. For your inner child to be met in this way, after all this time, will feel truly transformative for him or her ... and for you. Inner child work is something I have experienced from both sides of the couch, as the therapist and as the client. Both experiences equally powerful, both experiences equally moving, both experiences equally beautiful. When it comes to meaningful deep healing work, inner child work is it, and throughout this Ten-Step Healing Journey, particularly when we visit Step Four Heal Your Inner Child, I will gently guide you on a journey to heal the terrified little boy or girl deep inside of you, and in turn heal your anxiety, stress and inner turmoil.

Throughout this journey we will connect on many levels with the younger versions of us we carry deep inside. We'll allow these younger versions of us to surface, and when they do, we will lovingly consider their needs and how our adult selves can honour them. We will also learn how to soothe and comfort our inner child when they are distressed as we connect with them through visualisations, meditations, written exercises and through reparenting them to offer them everything they once yearned for when they were most in need. As we complete this journey together I will guide you on how to keep your inner child and his or her needs close and how to listen out for them as they call on you. This journey will guide you to connect with your inner child daily, to soothe them often, and to nurture them. I really hope that connecting with your inner child is as powerful for you as it is for me, and that once introduced to this work on this level you continue to practise this inner child healing, returning to it as often as you need it. If there is one lesson inner child work has taught me, it is that no one else can soothe us or the chaos of our minds in the way we can soothe, love and care for ourselves.

TECHNIQUES TO CALM THE CHAOS
Let your mind and heart rest for a while. You will catch up, the world will not stop spinning for you, but you will catch up. Take a rest.
CYNTHIA GO

The world of psychology offers a multitude of wonderful techniques to calm the chaos of our minds as it engulfs us. I love many of these techniques, especially for in-the-moment soothing, and find them very powerful, particularly when intrusive thoughts or catastrophising hits. Below I'll introduce you to some of my favourite techniques, which I turn to day in, day out, both in my therapy room and in my own healing practice.

Learning Note: Intrusive thoughts are disturbing thoughts that pop into your mind, without invitation or warning, that are usually very different from your typical thoughts. Intrusive thoughts will usually feel bothersome and hard to control or rid your mind of, and are often repetitive in nature. They can appear out of nowhere, can be violent or sexual, and can focus on behaviours you find completely unacceptable and abhorrent. However, intrusive thoughts have no meaning in your life. They are not warning messages or red flags. They are simply thoughts. What gives intrusive thoughts power is that those who experience them can become worried about their significance and can fixate on them and become ashamed, intent on keeping them secret from others. As long as someone experiencing intrusive thoughts can recognise that these are thoughts and thoughts alone, and that just because they think them doesn't mean they have any desire to act on them, intrusive thoughts aren't harmful in any way.

Catastrophising, in contrast, is a thought pattern or cognitive distortion individuals can experience that leads them to imagine, and indeed believe, that the worst-case scenario is about to, or will, happen.

When my anxiety was at its worst, my entire day was consumed by it. From the moment I woke until last thing at night, my mind would be circling and swirling, full of 'what ifs' and catastrophic, intrusive thoughts. Something as simple as my boyfriend going on a night out would cause me huge distress; my body would be on high alert, my thoughts would be spiralling and I would feel sick to my stomach. Rationally, I knew this wasn't a life or death-style scenario, but my mind and body would be reacting as if it were. 'What is he doing? Is he holding me in mind or has he forgotten about me completely?'; 'What are the people he is with like? Are they nice, normal lads, or will he get caught up in their wildness?'; 'I wonder if he'll meet someone prettier/funnier/more interesting than me? It's not as if I have much to offer.' If I could I would organise my own fun on these occasions to take my mind off things, but on the nights I had no plans I'd sit at home completely overtaken by my anxiety. At its worst I couldn't even sleep on those nights or I'd wake up every hour to check my phone to see if he had sent me a 'I'm home now, sleep tight!' message. When this message eventually arrived, as it always did, the war inside my head would finally subside and I could relax, safe in the knowledge that all was as it should be, but until that moment the anxiety would be heightened beyond belief.

Utilising Worry Time to Quieten your Mind
Worry often gives a small thing a big shadow.
SWEDISH PROVERB

A really powerful technique I turned to that helped me on those debilitating and exhausting days and nights, and one I outline to all my clients, is Worry Time. The premise of Worry Time is to postpone your worry to one short period per day (for example, 10 to 15 minutes) and to allow your worry to circulate and swirl only within this time frame. For example, on the days where Paul had a night out planned, I would do my very best to limit my anxiety to my set Worry

Time. When this time of the day arrived, I would worry all I liked, letting my mind take the reins, but if I could, especially after spending lots of time building up this skill, I would 'manage' my anxiety outside this period. To help me with this I would often combine further techniques with my Worry Time (like those outlined below and in Step Three Regulate your Nervous System) or I would turn to distraction. Very simply put, distraction is a task you choose to engage in to distract your mind from your fear, such as reading a book, watching a movie, listening to a podcast, chatting to a friend, or going for a brisk walk. Worry Time really benefited me when I became au fait with incorporating it into my day, and gave me a real sense of having 'control' over my anxiety, which felt very empowering. If you would like to learn how to manage your anxiety in this way, here is how to begin:

Stage 1: To create Worry Time in your life, begin by selecting your worry period. Choose a time that makes sense for you and when you will be able to complete this exercise without distractions. This could be after you have your dinner every evening, or as part of your wind-down evening routine, but it is important that you are realistic and setting yourself up to succeed.

Stage 2: Once you have your Worry Time scheduled, throughout your day, when worry hits, notice it and acknowledge it, 'I feel you, I hear you, I know you are present for me', but postpone it until your allocated Worry Time, 'but I am choosing not to engage with this worry now. Instead I will engage with it during my allocated Worry Time.' In this moment, as best you can, continue with the task you were completing when your worry hit or soothe or distract yourself so you can push the worry that entered your mind to its designated time.

Stage 3: When your Worry Time arrives, in a space that feels safe and comfortable for you, allow yourself to engage with the worries that entered your head throughout the day. (When you begin to practise Worry Time, you may wish to note your worries on a piece of paper throughout the day and to bring this information to your designated Worry Time.) Within your allocated time frame, you are free to worry about as many of these points as you feel drawn to. If a particular worry has passed and is no longer a concern for you, cross it off your list and let it go. Once your Worry Time has come to an end, do something that signifies to you that your Worry Time is over (for example closing your notebook and putting it away, or getting into your pyjamas and lighting a candle to ease you into wind-down mode) and engage in something nurturing to switch your brain from Worry Time to the present moment. Offer yourself as much TLC as you need here, especially in the beginning as you build familiarity with this new technique, and be gentle with yourself in the process.

The Power of Journaling to Lower Distress

I wonder if there's enough paper in the world to hold what I need to say. I've been silent for so long.
JANE TEMPLE

In those really dark days and nights, journaling was without doubt one of my favourite anxiety- and stress-lowering techniques, and it is still one I turn to on an almost daily basis. As a psychologist I am often asked, 'But how do I actually journal? I hear the term all the time, but what does it actually entail?' The beauty of journaling is that it can take many forms:

- It could be a free flow of your thoughts or emotions as you put pen to paper with no other goal than to empty your mind or to bring awareness or understanding to the tangle in your head.

- It might be answering journal prompts you write for yourself or find online or in a book.

- It could be writing out each and every stressful To Do on paper so it has a home rather than circling around in your head. You can even use this list to schedule your To Dos, or to delete them, defer them, delegate them or list them as a priority.

- You could try gratitude journaling, which involves listing three or more precious things you appreciate from your day (or you may wish to add this step as part of another journaling method you are engaging in).

- You might feel drawn to writing a therapeutic letter you'll never send during a journaling session, for example to someone who has hurt you in the past or to someone you have lost in your life.

- Or you can document your high points or the things that are going really well for you.

When it comes to journaling there are no rules, so create journaling sessions that feel right for you and that you enjoy. Reap the rewards of this deeply healing technique and the release and freedom it brings.

HEALING EXERCISE

Complete this exercise at a time and in a place where you feel comfortable and safe and that is distraction-free.

Journal prompts to calm the chaos:

What would life be like if I had control over my anxiety, rather than it having control over me?

Deep down, the reason I experience chaos (or anxiety) in my mind (or in my life) is ...

If I could help someone understand the huge impact this has on my life they would know ...

The thing that would support me most with calming my chaos is ...

And this is how I can start achieving it ...

Challenging Anxious or Negative Thoughts

Everything can be taken from a man but ... the last of the human freedoms – to choose one's attitude in any given set of circumstances.
VIKTOR FRANKL

Recently I worked with a lovely client, Aimee. Often in my work I encounter women I could imagine being friends with if life had brought us together in a different way, and Aimee was without doubt one of these women. Not only was she beautiful on the outside, she was also a warm, loving and sensitive soul and from our sessions together I could imagine that she left the people in her life feeling brighter and more uplifted than she found them.

Aimee and I began working together a few weeks after she discovered her husband, the father of her children, had engaged in a long-term emotional affair with another woman, which had culminated in a night of physical intimacy. Aimee was distraught on learning this news and was battling with whether to stay in the relationship, as her husband was begging her to do, or to up and leave. After weeks of back and forth in her mind, Aimee made the brave decision to remain in the relationship and to work through the affair, while also taking steps to improve the way they were interacting and communicating as a couple, in the hope they could rebuild their marriage. This was working really well for Aimee and her husband, with the help of couples and individual therapy, and Aimee felt very confident that she had made the right decision in staying, both for herself and her young children. However, the one thing Aimee was really struggling with was her perception of how other people were viewing her: 'They must think I'm an idiot for staying'; 'I feel their judgement when I see them. It's horrible.'

As part of our work together, Aimee and I focused on these really challenging thoughts for a number of weeks. These thoughts, although very strong for Aimee, were perhaps not necessarily true. Aimee had no proof that the people in her life were judging her in this way; in fact, not one of the small circle of people Aimee and her husband had trusted enough to share their circumstances with had spoken to Aimee in this way. They were instead gathering around her, supporting and encouraging her and showering her with love.

This work focused on understanding where these thoughts might be coming from and, most importantly, challenging them. For example:

- *Is there evidence to support this thought?*

- *What is the evidence for and against this thought?*

- *Might there be another viewpoint that people are taking other than judging you and thinking you're 'an idiot'?*

- *How do you think you might view these people if the tables were turned?*

- *Do you think they may perhaps be viewing you in this way too?*

- *When you are interacting with these people, how do you feel in your gut they are perceiving you? (Deep in your gut, not based on the automatic negative thoughts that may be racing through your mind.)*

Challenging her thoughts in this way really helped Aimee to realise that there were parts of herself, deep within, that were judging and criticising her and that she was projecting on to these other people, but that in fact, no one else was treating her in this way and she had no evidence whatsoever to back up the automatic negative thoughts she was experiencing.

This same approach can be used when it comes to anxious chaotic thoughts, like: 'They haven't answered the phone, they should be home by now, they must have been in a terrible car accident,' or, 'They haven't replied to my message, they must no longer want to be in this relationship with me,' or, 'They never normally nap for this long, they could be dead in their cot.'

A really simple but effective way to challenge thoughts such as these, or any anxious thoughts that arise for you, is to answer questions such as those outlined above in Aimee's example:

- Is there any evidence to support this idea?

- What is the evidence for and against it?

- Are there other explanations or viewpoints?

- What is the worst that could happen, and how would I cope?

- What is the best that could happen?

- What outcome is most realistic?

- What is the result of such automatic negative thinking?

In the beginning, when you are building this new practice, putting pen to paper to answer these questions will be the most powerful for you, so this is how I recommend you engage in this incredibly helpful exercise. Take as long as you need to really work through these questions to challenge the anxious or unhelpful thoughts you are experiencing. Come back to this exercise time and again, so that it becomes an automatic support you turn to when you need it most. Science has shown the power of this work, and for countless years I have turned to this technique with clients in my therapy room. Challenging your thoughts in this way *will* change things for you hugely, this I promise you. It has worked so powerfully for me on both a professional and a personal level. Remember, just 'because you think it, it doesn't mean it is true'.

HEALING EXERCISE

Pause here to complete the questions above in relation to a recent anxious or unhelpful thought you have experienced. Feel the power of this exercise for yourself. This is the work, and it will benefit you immeasurably if you can commit to it as wholly as I and many of my clients have over the years.

And remember, nothing changes without making a change.

Turning to Self-Compassion to Calm the Chaos

When we open our hearts to what is, it generates a level of warmth that helps heal our wounds.
DR KRISTEN NEFF

Very simply put, self-compassion is the process of showering oneself with kindness, understanding and encouragement (and quietening the judgement and criticism that can be so automatic for us). Self-compassion comprises three main components:

1. Offering ourselves the same kindness, understanding and compassion we so easily and freely give to those around us.

2. Recognising our shared humanity and connection to others, in that none of us are perfect; we all struggle, make mistakes, and carry vulnerabilities and imperfections.

3. Taking a mindful approach to our struggles; leaning into the experience, accepting the struggle and supporting ourselves and our needs through it.

Not only does self-compassion help to lower self-judgement and criticism, it has also been found to lower anxiety and stress levels, increase optimism and overall wellbeing, and act as a buffer against distressing experiences such as trauma.

When lowering anxiety and stress through the healing power of self-compassion, the idea is to treat yourself with as much kindness and understanding as you would a loved one in distress.

REFLECTIVE PAUSE

Imagine a friend turned to you and shared that they had been feeling deeply anxious for the past few weeks. How would you meet them in this admission? Spend a moment considering this and perhaps even jotting down the thoughts that come to mind.

> Now spend a moment considering how you would most likely meet *yourself* while experiencing similar distress. Again, reaching for a pen to jot down the thoughts that come to mind may heighten the power of this reflective moment for you.
>
> Finally, spend a moment connecting with something that has caused you stress or anxiety this week. With this situation in mind, imagine offering yourself the same understanding, kindness and support you so freely offer to your loved ones. How does this feel? Spend some time sitting with this kindness and understanding, again perhaps putting pen to paper, and pay attention to how treating yourself in this way feels for you.

Turning to self-compassion hugely changed my relationship with myself. Prior to being introduced to this healing practice I would judge and criticise myself so cruelly. On those nights I felt so anxious that I couldn't sleep I would berate myself for feeling how I did; 'You are so pathetic, look at the anxious mess that you are, for God's sake get over it.' Even sharing this deeply personal story with you now feels exposing, and I won't lie, as I type I wonder how I may be perceived in sharing myself in such a vulnerable light, but when I meet this part of myself with self-compassion, the fear dissipates; 'It's okay for you to feel this way. You felt anxious on all those nights all those years ago because of the early wounds you carry. Pain impacts us all, and anxiety is a part of many people's life. Go gently and be kind to yourself.'

Due to the profoundly healing power self-compassion has had in my life, I feel so passionately about its benefits that it features as a step of its own along the healing journey we are embarking on together. So for now, continue navigating Step Two Calm the Chaos of your Mind exactly as you are, while also looking forward to Step Six Cultivate Compassion, which you will soon reach.

STEP TWO CALM THE CHAOS OF YOUR MIND SUMMARY

So much of the distress and dis-ease the people I cross paths with experience in their lives is due to the chaos they witness in their minds. Chaos from never-ending To Do lists and from constantly juggling too many balls; chaos from catastrophising and fear of the unknown; chaos from interacting with people in ways that feel uncomfortable or unfamiliar, or when putting themselves out there in life and taking risks to follow their dreams; chaos from stress and anxiety – that is incredibly prevalent, especially since the pandemic and with all that has been happening in the world since; chaos from the early wounds and traumas we have experienced that still impact us, even to this day. Throughout Step Two Calm the Chaos of Your Mind we have looked at incredibly powerful ways to do just that, calm the chaos, from engaging in therapy and inner child work to soothing ways to calm anxiety, stress and fear through journaling, incorporating Worry Time, challenging negative thoughts, offering yourself self-compassion, and more. I really hope that the concepts, methods and techniques I have introduced you to throughout Step Two Calm the Chaos of Your Mind help to bring you deep peace in understanding why it feels like your mind is constantly in chaos and in how you can meaningfully change this, through quietening your stress, anxiety, catastrophising and intrusive thoughts. All the exercises I have laid out for you throughout Step Two are shared in the hope that you will try them, and in doing so, witness their power; and that you will be inspired to continue using these practices along your healing journey. By doing so, you will undoubtedly calm the chaos of your mind and find deep inner peace and balance.

Note: For years my anxiety ruled me. During this time, when I turned to my favourite anxiety-calming techniques, they without doubt soothed and benefited me. However, it is important for me to note that it was only when I truly dived into the deep wounds that were the underlying cause of my anxiety, in therapy and through inner child work, that deep healing came. The above techniques are powerful and work wonders for taking control of your anxiety, but the deep inner work that comes with understanding our traumas and how to heal from them are the work that most untangles the hold these wounds have on our lives and the impact they have on us.

STEP THREE

REGULATE YOUR NERVOUS SYSTEM

Look to the nervous system as the key to maximum health.
GALEN

Allow me to introduce you to Alice. Alice was an incredibly successful woman in her mid-thirties when she first contacted me to engage in weekly therapy. Alice was creative, vibrant, passionate and highly intelligent. She had transformed her business from a wishful dream she held in her heart to an award-winning million-euro entity. Alice put everything she had into her business: she was the founder, director, head marketer and publicist, front of house, admin co-ordinator, buyer and strategist all wrapped up in one. Her phone was constantly in reach, and even on her 'out of office' days she would check in to make sure all was in order and that there were no fires to extinguish. In my first session with Alice she spoke about how on edge she felt. All. The. Time. She shared the constant pressure. The headaches. The tension. The back pain. The stomach issues. The anxiety and stress. She also spoke about feeling so disconnected from everyone and everything and how over the past number of years she felt she was working all the time and so had absolutely no personal life. In response to Alice's distress I introduced her to the concept of a dysregulated nervous system and the astronomical impact that this can have on us, mind, body and soul. Alice's jaw dropped in that session; 'How are we not taught about this in school? It makes so much sense when you break it down in this way. I never knew this was happening for me but you've absolutely hit the nail on the head.'

For a number of months Alice and I worked together to understand and challenge her behaviour, getting to the root cause of why she always pushed herself so hard and how she could begin to invite change into her life and so live a calmer, more peaceful existence. As part of this work Alice was able to identify that having felt like she had let her parents down once before, and never wanting to be in that position again, she pushed herself to the brink with her work. This was coupled with being parentified as a child when her neurotic mother was unable to bear the load and her gentle but emotionally absent father was metaphorically out of sight. With these realisations and her new-found understanding of her exhaustion, we slowly began working on regulating Alice's nervous system and creating a life that felt more balanced and inviting for her. Initially Alice pushed against this because living her life in such a controlled and fast-paced way was so familiar for her. Let's face it, it was absolutely serving her in that her business was booming. However, now that the fog had cleared for Alice she could very clearly see the damage her lifestyle was having on her, both physically and mentally, and resolutely felt unable to continue living in this way.

Over the course of our time together Alice completely transformed her life and everything changed for her. Her stomach pain vanished. Her tension dissipated. Her anxiety and stress diminished. She even took an entire three-month sabbatical from her business, which she initially planned to 'use wisely', but at the end of her time off, when we met for a check-in session, Alice admitted that she had actually done very little in those three months, apart from living a slow and nurturing life. Exactly what the doctor ordered and a wise use of her time indeed.

So how, like Alice, do we regulate our nervous system? Let's look at the science and break it down so you too can experience Alice's 'Aha!' moment.

REGULATING YOUR NERVOUS SYSTEM THROUGH STRENGTHENING THE VAGUS NERVE

The vagus nerve is the conductor of the human body symphony orchestra.
NAVAZ HABIB

When it comes to regulating our nervous system to calm the chaos of our minds, and in turn, our anxiety and stress, it is important to understand our bodies' autonomic nervous system and how it functions, so let's take a look.

Our autonomic nervous system is our body's command centre. It originates in our brain, and controls our movements, thoughts and automatic responses to the world around us. Our autonomic nervous system also controls other body systems and processes, such as digestion and breathing, and regulates our automatic bodily functions. This system of our body is separated into two branches: our parasympathetic nervous system and our sympathetic nervous system. The parasympathetic nervous system controls our body's ability to relax. You may have heard the parasympathetic nervous system being referred to as the 'rest and digest' system; it regulates and relaxes us after a sense of threat has passed (whether this was a real threat or an imagined threat). In addition, our parasympathetic nervous system helps our body to maintain important daily functions like our resting heart rate, our metabolism and our breathing rate.

The other branch of our autonomic nervous system is the sympathetic nervous system, which is involved in stimulating areas of the body when facing stressful situations, especially during the fight, flight, freeze or fawn response. Typically how this works is that when we perceive a stressor (like a real or imagined threat), our sympathetic nervous system kicks in and we prepare to fight, freeze, flee or fawn. In an ideal situation, once the danger subsides, the parasympathetic branch of the nervous system is activated and our heart and breathing rate decrease; our digestion restarts; and all our other bodily functions go back to their normal level as we switch into 'rest and digest' mode as our stress response and 'DANGER' alarm signal is deactivated. However, sometimes this does not happen and we continue to remain in stress response mode even when the threat has vanished. This can happen when we are living in a long-term state of stress where cortisol and adrenaline constantly flood our body, leaving us feeling on edge and in a constant state of hypervigilance (just as Alice was). This is why it can sometimes feel hard to relax and wind down, especially at night, and also why it is so important to learn ways to soothe and regulate ourselves to calm our minds.

THE VAGUS NERVE

This is where the vagus nerve comes in to play. Approximately 75 per cent of all parasympathetic nerves link to form something called the vagus nerve. The vagus nerve has branches in many key organs, such as the stomach, kidneys, bladder and reproductive organs. It plays numerous important roles, including communication between the brain and the gut; decreasing inflammation; lowering the heart rate and blood pressure; and fear management.

The vagus nerve sends information to brain regions important in anxiety and stress regulation (e.g. the locus coeruleus, orbitofrontal cortex, insula, hippocampus and amygdala), and over the last number of decades this pathway has been targeted in efforts to alleviate symptoms of anxiety and stress. Efforts mainly focus on stimulating the vagus nerve to increase vagal tone. Think of building your biceps by consistently lifting weights. This is the same as building vagal tone; the more we exercise or stimulate this nerve with activities that strengthen it, the more it activates the parasympathetic nervous system, bringing us into 'rest and digest' or getting us there faster. Having higher vagal tone means that your body can relax much faster and far more easily after experiencing anxiety and stress and that you are equipped to bring your mind from chaos to calm.

So how do we increase vagal tone?

1. Cold exposure. Acute cold exposure has been shown to activate the vagus nerve. Researchers have found that regularly exposing yourself to cold temperatures can lower your sympathetic fight, flight, freeze or fawn response and increase parasympathetic activity through the vagus nerve. Think cold showers (start at 10 seconds and increase their duration), ice baths, going outside in cold temperatures with minimal clothing or simply submerging your face in ice-cold water or your body in the sea (one of my favourite wellness rituals!).

2. Deep breathing. Deep breathing is another way to stimulate your vagus nerve, and it has been shown to reduce anxiety and stress and to increase the parasympathetic system by activating the vagus nerve. Most people take about ten to fourteen breaths each minute, but aiming to take about six breaths over the course of a minute is a great way to relieve stress. To do this, breathe in deeply from your diaphragm and expand your stomach outwards. Your exhale should be long and slow. This is key to stimulating the vagus nerve and reaching a state of relaxation. Once you get comfortable with this, consider introducing 'the physiological sigh' into your deep breathing toolkit. This is where you inhale, inhale again, and release a long, and slow exhalation. This was one of Alice's favourites!

3. Singing, humming, chanting and gargling. The vagus nerve is connected to our vocal cords and the muscles at the back of our throat. Singing, humming, chanting and gargling can activate these muscles and stimulate our vagus nerve to increase vagal tone and, in turn, calm anxiety or stress. Music can also bring us into a state of calm, so this one is a double whammy for music lovers!

4. Probiotics. It is becoming increasingly clear to researchers that healthy gut bacteria improve brain function by affecting the vagus nerve, so it may be time to consider starting a new probiotic.

5. Meditation. Meditation is one of my favourite relaxation techniques and it has been found to stimulate the vagus nerve and increase vagal tone. Research shows that meditation also increases positive emotions and promotes feelings of goodwill towards oneself and others, and reduces sympathetic fight, flight, freeze or fawn activity, which increases vagal modulation.

Exercise, journaling, progressive muscle relaxation, spending time with loved ones, laughter, dancing, massage and taking omega-3 fatty acids have also been found to stimulate the vagus nerve and improve vagal tone, and to lower anxiety, stress and overwhelm, so when it comes to regulating your nervous system, there really is a way to do so for everyone. The key here is trying them out and finding your favourite so that you can build it into your lifestyle in an achievable and consistent way. Continue reading to find out exactly how.

When it comes to implementing an activity in your life to strengthen your vagal tone and regulate your nervous system by helping it to switch more easily and more frequently from the sympathetic (fight, flight, freeze, fawn), to the parasympathetic (rest and digest), the magic happens when you *consistently* practise your chosen activity, time and time again. Rather than picturing this journey as a mountain you have to move, imagine that it is a pile of small pebbles and boulders, and that day by day, as you engage in your chosen activity, you are lifting these pebbles and boulders one by one. In time the mountain will have vanished and you will be free to pass, stronger and more resilient than you have ever been before.

To do this, trial whichever of the above exercises you feel drawn to. Once you've selected your favourite, and the one you most believe you will be able to stick to, write out your nervous system regulation plan. This plan will consist of your chosen activity, the number of days per week you plan to carry it out, and the time each day you will do so. To give yourself the best chance, I recommend scheduling these events in your diary or your phone's calendar and following through with your plan to the best of your ability. To further support your consistency, attach the activity to an anchor that is already present in your day, like when you wake up in the morning or get into bed in the evening, or before you have your lunch. A really strong anchor in my day is when my children go to bed, and that's when I get into my pyjamas and do my skincare routine; so for me this would be an excellent time to do my chosen activity. (My favourites are meditating, journaling and progressive muscle relaxation (PMR). As a bonus, I always focus on my breath while meditating and practising PMR, so it's a double whammy!) Last but not least, while building this consistency in your life, try setting an alarm to remind you of your daily 'date'; that way you have no excuse!

HEALING EXERCISE

Practise this exercise in a safe space free from distraction. Get cosy, grab your favourite blanket and relax into the chair, mat, floor or bed supporting your body. Settle in for a healing journey.

One powerful way I lower my anxiety when it arrives and switch from 'fight or flight' into 'rest and digest' is to breathe into the emotions and sensations I am experiencing to create safety within my mind, body and soul and to help me (and my nervous system) return to calm. Let's give this a try together in the hope that it brings you as much calm as it does me. I really hope it does.

First, take a moment to pause and to breathe. If it feels safe to do so, close your eyes and gently bring your awareness to your breath.

Inhale deeply from the base of your belly, slow and steady deep breaths in and out, in and out, in and out. Notice how your body begins to respond to this perfect stillness.

Now I invite you to bring your hand to your heart and lovingly place it against your chest.

Feel the rhythm that welcomes you here.

You are safe.

All is well.

There is nothing for you to do in the moment, except be.

Continue to breathe as you connect with your heart.

Inhale deeply, and let go.

Inhale deeply, and let go.

Inhale deeply, and let go.

Take a few more moments here to rest and to enjoy the sensations that arise and the peace that comes.

As you engage in this gentle stillness, it's time now to let go.

To let go of all that you have been carrying, for you are tired.

It's time to let go of all of the thoughts you have been trying to hold on to.

It's time to let go of all of the worries you have been carrying on your shoulders.

It's time to let go of all of your fears.

It is now time to rest.

As you feel your body starting to relax, you see a beautiful flight of stairs in front of you. Maybe they are familiar to you, or perhaps you have never seen them before. Whichever it is for you, these stairs are waiting for you, shimmering, calling you forward, calling you to descend, and so you choose to step onto the staircase, beginning with the first stair, then you take a second, feeling the touch of the step beneath your feet, and then you move on to each step below, noticing how you feel as you slowly descend.

There are ten steps altogether, so go ahead and allow yourself to take one step at a time, all the way to the bottom, as each step brings you deeper inside yourself.

When you get to step number ten you notice in front of you the most amazing door. You instantly know that the space behind the door is for you and that it is filled with unconditional love, inspiration and guidance, and so you go ahead, you open the door, you step into the brightly lit space, closing the door behind you as you step in in your entirety.

Before you lies the most glorious, serene beach you've ever seen. It is so perfect that it takes your breath away. Let yourself feel and see and sense this beautiful beach. The gentle breeze on your skin, the powder-soft sand beneath your feet, the sound of the waves as they lap on the shore, the heat of the sun on your skin.

The light is so bright and holds so much love. The temperature is just perfect and it feels as though every pore of your being is having this glorious light being poured into it, being nourished, being revitalised.

Continue with your deep inhalations and exhalations and let yourself be nourished by this light as you walk towards the seashore and watch as the water sparkles and shimmers in the sun. It is so peaceful here and as you stand on the water's edge you sigh out a breath of relaxation, you feel so at home, so content, so at peace.

As you soak in the beauty that surrounds you, you lower yourself onto the sand to rest for a while. You close your eyes, turn your face to the sun, and continue to breathe in and out the peace and calm that envelops you, slowly and deeply.

As you rest, your body feels so relaxed, so at peace, so free.

When you feel ready to continue your journey you open your eyes, drinking in the shimmering waves and smiling to yourself. As you do this you notice by your side a beautiful box. You touch the box, admiring its design and colour, and as you connect with it, you realise exactly why it has arrived for you. This box is a gift, and one that has come for you to place in it all that you need to let go of.

As this awareness comes, so too does the knowledge and reassurance that this box can fit everything you need it to. All you need to do is to trust, and so you do.

Go ahead and spend some time contemplating all that you need to let go of. All that you have been carrying, all that has been holding you back. Take this at your own pace. We have all the time in the world.

As you look at this box on the shore beside you, full of all that you have needed to let go of, your body feels so light, so at peace, so free. You feel so grateful to have received this gift of letting go. It has felt so powerful and so needed.

When you feel ready, you stand up and gently push your box and all that it holds into the shimmering water. It floats away from you, and you watch as it gets smaller and smaller as it travels. The further it goes, the lighter and more at peace you feel. You smile to yourself, knowing you have let go of so much.

You feel so relaxed.

So at peace.

So calm.

As you stand here on this amazing seashore watching your box fade away into the sunset you visualise yourself taking a step back from all of the things that have been burdening you that you have just freed yourself from.

Really picture this in your mind.

Take a step back and let it all go.

Lay it all down, as now it is time for you to rest.

As you pause in this peaceful stillness, allow yourself to stop the doing, to stop the trying, to stop the holding so tightly on to everything because you are scared.

You are safe.

All is well.

There is nothing for you to do in the moment, except be.

Perhaps now is a good time to listen.

To listen to your heart.

To listen to your soul.

To listen to your inner wisdom.

It is only when we pause to listen that we can realign to our true selves.

For you carry everything you need within you.

Including the power to ground and calm and soothe you and your nervous system when you are feeling anxious, overwhelmed or dysregulated.

Whenever you need this support, it is here. Deep within.

Take as long here as you need, enjoying the peace and calm that comes.

Before you turn to begin your journey home, for one last moment you enjoy the sights ... sounds ... and smells of this perfect beach that has offered you so much.

You feel the sun, warm on your skin.

You feel the gentle breeze blow across your cheek.

You feel the powder-soft sand beneath your feet.

You turn, and begin your journey home, finding yourself back at your beautiful door, and when you are ready you open it, and one by one, you walk back up your shimmering staircase.

As you walk, step by step by step, your body slowly begins to reawaken.

Know that you can return to this beautiful staircase and to your beautiful beach whenever you need to and whenever you like.

As you reawaken, keep with you the feeling of calm, peace, and relaxation.

Wiggle your fingers and toes to wake up your muscles.

Shrug your shoulders. Stretch for a while if your body feels called to do so.

And when you are ready, open your eyes and return to the space you are in feeling relaxed, so light, and so at peace.

This powerful meditation is one I use regularly with my clients, and one they go on to practise outside our sessions. This is one I too use when I'm feeling anxious, overwhelmed or when my mind needs some nurturing calmness. I really hope this deeply healing meditation is as powerful for you and that you choose to practise it, returning to it as often as you need it.

GROUNDING TECHNIQUES TO LOWER ANXIETY, STRESS AND OVERWHELM AND TO REGULATE YOUR NERVOUS SYSTEM

It is only by grounding our awareness in the living sensation of our bodies that the 'I am', our real presence, can awaken.
G.I. GURDJIEFF

Recently I had one of those days where it felt like everything that could go wrong did go wrong, and as though I was in firefighting mode all day. My stress levels were at an all-time high and I could feel my anxiety rapidly heightening too as more and more adrenaline and cortisol was released into my bloodstream and as my body remained in fight or flight mode all day. At one stage my husband handed me some chocolate and told me to eat it. I'm not sure if he thought I needed the sugar for energy after all the running around I was doing or because he wanted to quieten my panicked complaining, at least for a couple of minutes. (Whatever his reasoning, I ate the chocolate!) I'm sharing this story with you, because it's days like these that are the perfect time to turn to grounding techniques to calm, soothe, and, well, ground you.

So what exactly are grounding techniques? They're actions you complete to bring yourself into contact with the present moment and to instil calm when you need it most (like when your mind is racing, when you're feeling really heightened physiologically, or when your breath is shallow and irregular). Grounding techniques can be quick simple techniques like taking three slow deep breaths in through your nose and out through your mouth, or using your senses to pull you back into the present moment; or longer techniques, like a body scan meditation or progressive muscle relaxation (one of my favourites).

Different grounding techniques work for different people, and there is no right or wrong way to ground yourself. The important thing to remember is that the main aim when practising grounding techniques is to connect your mind and body to the present moment. This will help calm you and, most importantly, your nervous system, so that you can lower those anxious and stressful feelings you are experiencing. As well as being helpful for situations where you find yourself feeling overwhelmed or anxious, grounding techniques can also be incredibly helpful for times you feel impacted by distressing memories, thoughts and feelings.

Here are four of my favourite grounding techniques. I hope they bring as much peace and harmony to your life as they bring to mine.

DEEP BREATHING

Sit comfortably and allow yourself to be still. Close your eyes if this feels comfortable for you (this is my preferred way) or fix your gaze on something static in front of you. Now gently take a slow deep breath in through your nose all the way from your belly, and, just as slowly and gently, release this breath through your nose or mouth in a steady stream. Repeat nine times (or just twice if you're short on time, for example if you're about to start an exam or presentation – this is the joy of breathing;

you can do it anywhere and everywhere and no one will notice). Throughout this exercise, focus your mind on your breathing and feel your body relax, your mind slow, and the tension flow from your muscles.

USE YOUR SENSES TO GROUND YOU

If you're feeling overwhelmed, a simple but powerful way to ground and bring yourself back to the present moment is by using your senses. To begin, slowly notice, name and describe five things you can see, four things you can touch, three things you can hear, two things you can smell and one thing you can taste. Really lean into these sensations as you connect with them, elongating your experience of them and your focus. Do your best to connect with them in a way you have never done before and to sense them as deeply and as vibrantly as you can. In this exercise, touch is particularly grounding. Feel the wooden arm of your chair in your grip, or the cool metal of your phone. Feel the smooth paper of your diary or the ceramic of your mug. Connect with your senses and allow them to draw you back to earth and to calm and soothe any distressing or uncomfortable feelings you may be experiencing.

HEALING EXERCISE

Pause to complete the above exercise before reading on. Engage in it to the best of your ability and really soak in the power of your senses to gently but powerfully bring you into the here and now. Pay attention to how this activity is for you. Does it come naturally? Do you enjoy it? Is it something you feel you will reach for when anxiety or stress next surfaces for you? There are no rights or wrongs here, only learnings.

PLAY A MENTAL GAME

I use this grounding technique all the time when I'm lying in bed and finding it hard to relax my mind enough to drift off to sleep. I have different versions, but the premise is simple. Play a mental game that occupies your mind and grounds you to the present moment. One of my favourite versions is to list as many characters as possible from a book I recently read or a TV series I recently watched. Another option is the alphabet game, where you choose a topic, for example movies or fruit, and list one per letter from A to Z. If you're out and about you can set yourself a challenge like spotting five white cars within a certain time frame, or counting the number of red cars that you pass (my daughters love joining in on this one!).

PROGRESSIVE MUSCLE RELAXATION

Progressive muscle relaxation (or PMR) is a relaxation technique that involves tightening and relaxing your muscles, one at a time, in a strategic and specific order. The aim of this exercise is to ground and relax your mind, body and soul, while recognising any tension you may be carrying in your body, and releasing it. PMR has been found to be extremely beneficial in lowering anxiety, stress and overwhelm and in bringing calm and peace to busy minds through regulating the nervous system. It has also been found to improve sleep, and one of my favourite places to practise this exercise is in bed, last thing at night. It makes me feel as if I'm floating and it deeply relaxes me before it is time to fall asleep.

HEALING EXERCISE

Practise this exercise in a safe space free from distractions. Get cosy, grab your favourite blanket and relax into the chair, mat, floor or bed supporting your body. Settle in for a healing journey.

To begin, sit or lie in a comfortable position. Really allow yourself to sink into the support beneath your body. This is your time. To pause. To rest. To relax. To let go. If it feels safe to do so, close your eyes or, if you prefer, fix your gaze on something static in front of you. Do what feels most comfortable for you. There is nothing for you to do in this moment but be.

As you rest in this moment, take a slow, deep breath in through your nose and out through your mouth. On your next breath, as you exhale, sigh out any stress or tension you are holding in your body.

And again.

Feel the tension leaving your body and the peace and calmness that arrives.

Bring your attention now to your head and as best you can, tense or scrunch up your facial muscles as tightly as possible, hold for a count of five, and gently release.

Notice the tension melting away and the wave of peace that arrives.

Next move your head forwards or backwards and hold it in this pose, feeling the stretch and tension in your neck that arrives as you do so. Hold this position for a count of five, and gently release.

Feel the relaxation that arrives. Soak it in. Enjoy this moment.

Move your focus to your shoulders. As best as you can, lift and scrunch them up to your ears or bring your shoulder blades together behind you, feeling the tension and tightness that arrives in doing so. Hold for a count of five, and release.

Sit in the melting of your tension as your muscles relax. Pause here for a moment, allowing yourself to rest.

I invite you now to tense your biceps and the palms of your hands, squeezing as tightly as possible and holding this pose for a count of five, before gently releasing.

Notice the flow of energy throughout your arms and hands and the lightness that replaces the tension.

Next squeeze your abdominal muscles as tightly as you can. Hold for a count of five, and release.

Relax into the feeling of release that ensues. Enjoy this wonderful feeling you have created.

Bring your attention now to your sitting bones and clench as tightly as possible here, incorporating as much tension as you can. Hold for a count of five, and release.

Enjoy the new sensations that float throughout your body.

Focus now on your thigh muscles, squeezing as tightly as you can and really feeling the burn as you hold for a count of five. And release, enjoying the melting sensation that arrives for you.

Next raise your heels and squeeze your calf muscles with as much force as your body allows. Hold for a count of five. Now relax those muscles and your ankles.

Rest here for a moment enjoying the sensation that arrives.

As we bring our focus to our feet, scrunch them as tightly as you can, curling in your toes and feeling the tension that surrounds the muscles. Hold for a count of five and release.

Finally, with everything you have left within you, tightly squeeze in unison all the muscles of your body. Hold for a count of five, and release, enjoying the floating sensation that takes over your entire body.

Breathe out another slow, deep breath, and rest here awhile, enjoying all the benefits this relaxation exercise brings.

When you feel ready to do so, begin slowly waking your body to the space around you. Wiggle your fingers and toes and slowly arrive back to this moment and the here and now. Enjoy the gorgeous feelings of relaxation you have invited in and know that you can return to this feeling anytime your heart desires.

TECHNIQUES THAT SOOTHE AND INVITE CALM

Freedom is not given to us by anyone; we have to cultivate it ourselves. It is a daily practice ... No one can prevent you from being aware of each step you take or each breath in and breath out.
THICH NHAT HANH

Recently I held the most wonderful day retreat for 25 incredible women. It was one of those days when the group instantly gelled. We arrived as strangers, and within minutes came together as soul sisters. We laughed, we cried, we bared our souls, and we nourished and nurtured ourselves from the inside out. Everyone shared their story that day, from mothers who felt completely and utterly dysregulated, to trauma survivors, to those supporting and caring for others, to those grieving or finding their way through fertility journeys, to those navigating burnout, anxiety, depression and chronic pain. What almost every single woman shared that day was how hard it was to invite moments of peace and calm into their days, especially moments that actually lasted. After exploring this throughout the day, and the reasons why, one mother very quietly shared, 'But I just feel so anxious in my body all the time. I'm always on edge. I'm always primed to jump and put out the fire, even when there is no fire to distinguish. I'm always switched on and on high alert. It's exhausting and I don't know what to do. I shout at my children every night at bedtime and then cry myself to sleep afterwards because they don't deserve it, it's just me feeling so unable to keep my cool while I try to get them down every night.' As I listened to this gorgeous woman speaking, I noticed that many of the women sitting in our circle were nodding along and that one or two had tears streaming down their faces. This woman's story was so familiar to them, whether they had children or not.

'It sounds like you are constantly feeling dysregulated,' I said gently. She nodded as her own tears arrived. 'What can I do? I can't continue living in this way,' words that reminded me so much of Alice. We spoke that afternoon about self-soothing and about the importance of introducing pockets of calm into each and every day to regularly bring our nervous system from fight or flight into rest and digest. We spoke about how hard it can be to prioritise ourselves and put ourselves on our own To Do list and to nurture and nourish ourselves, free of guilt, despite the million and one other things circling around in our heads.

Self-soothing refers to any behaviour an individual uses to regulate their emotional state and their nervous system. As adults this can feel foreign, especially when it is a process or way of thinking that feels very unfamiliar. A simple way to bring this concept to life is to imagine the ways we try to soothe, calm and comfort an upset child. Self-soothing is just that, except we offer this love, comfort and care to ourselves (and the little girl or boy inside us). People choose to self-soothe in many ways. Something I see in many of my clients, and indeed which I of course engage in myself on occasion, is self-soothing through food, alcohol, scrolling on a phone or immersing oneself in the latest binge-worthy TV show. However, something I strongly urge you to consider is which self-soothing techniques bring you peace, comfort and a sense of relief (versus the ones we may automatically turn to, yet afterwards regret or don't truly receive any benefit from). We've all been there: suddenly the share-size bar of chocolate or bag of nachos is gone, yet we still feel the distress that led us there in the first place, or the regret of the morning after when alongside our anxiety we are also navigating a pounding headache.

For me, the self-soothing processes that bring the most comfort and peace to my life are things like:

- Sea swimming (often I set an intention for myself as I enter the water and imagine the process cleansing me and freeing me from whatever it is that I am aiming for)

- Drinking cacao and leaning into the power and healing that this plant medicine offers my body

- Meditating

- Going for a walk in nature

- Journaling

- Reading a good book

- Having a candle-lit bath

- Sharing how I feel with a loved one and asking for a hug

- Prioritising rest and 'me time'
- Listening to soothing music
- Burning relaxing essential oils, incense or palo santo
- Progressive muscle relaxation
- Using my senses to ground me to the current moment
- Allowing myself to slow down and to say 'No'
- Engaging in gentle somatic techniques
- Pausing to consider my needs and how I can offer myself this gift. (My needs may be rest, sleep, nourishment, hydration, alone time or to take pressure off myself.)

REFLECTIVE PAUSE

As you sit here reading my words, pause to consider the self-soothing techniques that offer you comfort, release, relief and peace (or self-soothing techniques you've never tried yet feel would strongly benefit you).

Pause here to consider this, before reading on.

As my beautiful retreat came to a close that day, the wonderful women who had gathered with me left with a new promise to themselves: to create pockets of calm and rest in their days to nurture and nourish both themselves and their nervous systems. They departed that deeply healing waterside haven determined to prioritise one ten-minute pause each and every day and to fill this time with a technique that would strengthen their vagus nerve while also bringing calm into their lives. They left appreciating that to truly regulate themselves and bring themselves into rest and digest mode they had to consistently introduce moments of calm into their lives, which would lead to their brains seeking out these moments more and more (by activating the brain's reward system). They left too with a desire to build new and healing neural pathways and habits, and to strengthen their vagal tone and vagus nerve, which would bring them back into rest and digest from fight or flight mode much more easily and more frequently; all of which would completely transform their lives. What a gift those gorgeous women gave to themselves that day, and what a gift you too can offer yourself. Something to consider, as if you would truly like to make a difference to your life, prioritising your nervous system is it.

SOMATIC TECHNIQUES

The body always leads us home ... if we can simply learn to trust sensation and stay with it long enough for it to reveal appropriate action, movement, insight or feeling.
PAT OGDEN

Anyone who has ever worked with me will know my love affair with somatic techniques. I am obsessed! Simply put, somatic techniques are exercises that soothe, connect and sync our mind, body and soul and, in a very gentle and healing way, release stored energy within us. Every single one of us carries an innate knowledge of how to heal our pain through listening to our inner wisdom and guidance and the messages our body sends us. However, we often silence this wisdom or disconnect from it. Unlike animals, who naturally release tension and emotional energy rather than storing it in their bodies – through yawning, trembling, stretching and shaking – we often carry it deep within us for long periods of time. I adore somatic techniques and practise them often, especially when I am experiencing emotions that feel particularly challenging or heavy. Somatic techniques are deeply healing as they can help us, in a very powerful way, to release stagnant energy within us that is often hugely impacting us, usually unbeknownst to us, and in turn, calm the chaos of our bodies and minds, including extremely debilitating anxiety and stress.

If you would like to experience the power of these techniques for yourself, try my favourites with an open heart and an open mind. When doing so, create a safe and comforting atmosphere for yourself, perhaps through dimming the lights, burning your favourite candles or essential oils, playing soft relaxing music and making sure you are warm and cosy. This is transformative work and deeply healing.

Connect with Your Breath and Your Heart

Stand, sit or lie in a space that feels comfortable. Begin by connecting with your breath. Breathe slow and steady deep breaths in a rhythm that feels soothing for you, and as you do so place one hand on your heart and one on your belly, or both hands on your heart, while connecting with the natural rhythm of your body. As you rest here in this moment, enjoy the sensations that arise for you, allowing yourself to give in to any feelings that may surface. Introduce a gentle sway from side to side to deepen this practice and stay in this moment for as long as feels soothing and beneficial for you.

Butterfly Tapping Sequence

Stand, sit or lie in a space that feels comfortable. Begin by connecting with your breath. Breathe slow and steady deep breaths in a rhythm that feels soothing for you, and as you do so place both hands in front of your chest, fingers pointing upwards and palms turned towards you. Cross your hands over as if creating a V shape with them and interlock your thumbs (if your hands are in the correct position they should resemble a butterfly). Place your hands against your chest in this position and slowly and rhythmically begin tapping them against your body, one at a time. Continue this bilateral movement of your hands, where one hand taps your chest, followed by the other, in a continual movement. As you engage in this gentle tapping process, notice any sensations that arrive for you and enjoy the relaxation and grounding that occurs.

Offer Yourself a Loving Butterfly Hug

Stand, sit or lie in a space that feels comfortable. Begin by connecting with your breath. Breathe slow and steady deep breaths in a rhythm that feels soothing for you, and as you do so place your left hand under your right armpit and your right hand on your left shoulder. When comfortable in this position, lovingly hold yourself as you offer yourself a warm hug. Use as much or as little pressure as feels soothing for you, and if you feel drawn to doing so, you can introduce a gentle sway from side to side to deepen this deeply soothing practice. Notice the sensations that arise for you as you offer yourself the gift of this nurturing and gentle moment.

Apply Gentle Pressure to Your Arms

Stand, sit or lie in a space that feels comfortable. Begin by connecting with your breath. Breathe slowly and steadily, deep breaths in a rhythm that feels soothing for you, and as you do so place your right hand on your left shoulder, and your left hand on your right shoulder. Slowly and gently apply pressure to the tops of your arms before moving your hands slightly down your biceps and repeating this gentle squeeze. Continue this sequence as you slowly work your hands all the way down your arms to your wrists, and just as slowly back up again towards your shoulders. Complete this exercise as many times as feels soothing for you, and as your body responds to this loving touch, enjoy any sensations that arrive.

Shake Your Body

Stand with your arms hanging loosely by your sides and your feet hip distance apart. In whatever way you feel called to do so, begin purposefully shaking your body, perhaps starting by rotating your shoulders and dropping this movement into shaking your arms, before moving on to shake one leg and then the other. Continue moving your body in this way for as long as you feel it is benefiting you, bringing your neck into the sequence too if rotating it feels soothing and comfortable. Enjoy the release this exercise brings as you feel the power of these movements flow through your body.

Be very gentle with yourself after engaging in these somatic techniques. Honour how you feel in the aftermath and offer yourself (and the little girl or boy within you) the tender loving care you would offer a loved one following a deeply moving healing release.

HEALING EXERCISE

Pause here to complete one of the incredibly powerful somatic techniques above before reading on. Engage in it to the best of your ability and really soak in the power moving your body in this way brings. Connect with your breath as you complete this technique and if you feel drawn to doing so, close your eyes and deeply feel the moment. I hope with all my heart you enjoy this experience as much as I do when I engage in somatic healing.

STEP THREE REGULATE YOUR NERVOUS SYSTEM SUMMARY

So much of my work focuses on helping people to live calmer, more peaceful lives. For me this is the ultimate goal: to feel calm, balanced and connected, both to myself and to those around me whom I love. Like my gorgeous client Alice, I too used to live a really busy life. I, like her, used to run from one task to the next, feeling that my To Do list was never diminishing, always growing. I lived my life putting out one fire after another and constantly promising myself that 'once I get to the end of this week things will be calmer', but this never rang true. My life was in a frenzy, and although to everyone on the outside looking in I likely appeared to have it all, I was falling to pieces, rushing around like a headless chicken. I too was the mother who blew up at bedtime after a day of dysregulation and who flopped on the couch at 9 p.m. too exhausted to do anything but watch mindless TV.

Making life feel easier, calmer and more manageable boils down in so many ways to how regulated our nervous system is. It is only through slowing down and learning to really nurture myself and my adrenaline and cortisol levels that life has changed for me. This has taken a lot of work, particularly in pushing through the fear that if I slow down or say 'No' opportunities will pass me by; however, the one huge change that has happened within me is that I'm finally okay with that. Instead of 'making a name for myself' and hoping to be called upon for every opportunity that arises, my goal now is peace and connection. So much so that there is nothing I love more than 'coming home to myself' and connecting inwards to my innate wisdom and soul whispers, especially as this means I am so much more resourced to take on life as a result. Life as a mother. Life as a psychologist. Life as a wife and daughter and friend. For example, just last week, at the worst time it could have possibly happened, my car had a puncture, but because life feels so much more manageable now I was able to remain calm, balanced and in control, rather than bursting into tears and feeling paralysed by my 'crisis'.

For my clients who wish the same for their lives, and for you, the greatest gift I can leave you with as we bring Step Three Regulate your Nervous System to a close, is to slow down through nurturing and honouring your nervous system. You might slow down in a big way, or in a small and simple yet consistent way. Only you know what you truly need to quieten the chaos of your body, mind and soul, but throughout Step Three I have shared with you how to do both. The only question now is are you willing to prioritise healing in your life? I really hope so.

STEP FOUR

HEAL YOUR INNER CHILD

She held herself until the sobs of the child inside subsided entirely. I love you, she told herself. It will all be okay.
H. RAVEN ROSE

Inside all of us lies an inner child. A little girl or boy who, for a lifetime, has felt scared, alone and not good enough. A little girl or boy who is yearning for love, comfort and connection. A little girl or boy who, when listened to and soothed, will transform your life.

Have you been listening to this little child deep inside you?

Inner child work is without doubt one of the most powerful healing modalities I have ever experienced in the therapy room. For countless years I have seen clients soothe their anxiety, pain and distress through connecting inward and offering their inner child what he or she is most yearning for. This may be love, comfort, gentle soothing, or simply to no longer feel alone. For your inner child to be met with this, after all this time, will feel truly transformative for him or her … and for you. I have experienced inner child work from both sides of the couch, as both therapist and client. Both experiences equally powerful, both experiences equally moving, both experiences equally beautiful. When it comes to meaningful deep healing work, inner child work is it, and throughout Step Four I will gently guide on a journey to heal your inner child. Are you ready?

> *When my father died, it felt like my entire world ended. I was 25 and knee-deep in all that the first year of a psychology doctorate brings. Essays, clinical formulations, client work, reflective diaries, group*

therapy and more. But suddenly, amidst all the busyness, amidst all the chaos, my father died, and in that moment my whole world stopped spinning. I felt so alone and so fearful in that deep abyss of grief. How could I go on without him? How could I go on when a part of me had also died?

I reverted to being a little girl. A little girl who yearned to be with him, cuddled up on his lap, snuggling into his safety and solidness. I longed to feel my hand in his while he told me that everything was going to be okay, as he had done so many times before. In the early days and weeks following his death, when I pictured him it was my father of years gone by, from when I was three and climbing on his back as he 'horsied' me to bed on all fours; from when I was five and pedalling furiously as he taught me how to ride my shiny new bicycle; from when I was seven and dressed all in white, twirling in my special dress, giggling.

When I thought of him in those first few days and weeks, I thought of him as 'Daddy'. I hadn't thought of him as Daddy or called him that for a very long time, but 'Daddy' now echoed in my mind with each memory of him that arose and each dream that came. On losing him, my inner child ruled me, desperately craving the safety he had always afforded, the safety I so innocently took for granted for so many years. Oh, how I wished I could go back in time and soak that in. Soak him in. Even now, 11 years on, when the tears arrive they arrive in floods, and each time my heart breaks all over again and I cry from deep within, from that little girl who has lost her daddy and wants nothing more than to see him and to have him tell her it's all going to be okay.

Does your inner child arise in you too?

When people hear the term 'inner child work' they often ask what it means and what it entails. Essentially, if we can learn to connect with and soothe our inner child (a younger version of ourselves we carry deep within us) when he or she becomes distressed, we will be able to soothe and regulate our adult selves.

Picture these scenarios:

- **Scenario One:** You've just had a blazing row with your partner and you feel completely dysregulated and scared that he or she will abandon you. You do everything you can to make up, apologising and taking all the blame, even though it's not all yours to claim.

- **Scenario Two:** While lounging on the couch on a random Saturday night you see a photo of your friends on social media enjoying a meal and a glass of wine together. You sit up quickly because you can't believe your eyes. No one invited you to this dinner. Tears start to build, your stomach starts to churn and you feel really left out.

- **Scenario Three:** Your best friend forgets your birthday. You can't believe you haven't heard from her and feel so let down. How could she forget? Does she not care about you? You go about your day and enjoy the effort other people make for you, but deep down your heart is heavy and you feel really emotional.

REFLECTIVE EXERCISE

What's common to all three of these scenarios?

Pause here to consider this question or to write some notes before reading on.

Pause too to consider if you've ever felt this way. Write about those times, allowing whatever arises within you to come. This is part of your healing process. Trust your inner knowing.

When I'm sad or angry or feeling really vulnerable you can be guaranteed that my inner child will come out in force. My emotions will be really heightened and instead of my logical adult self being in control, my inner five-year-old will be chaotically calling the shots. Usually when I become aware that this is happening (sometimes that can be immediate; sometimes, even with years of therapy behind me, it can take some time), it is a sign that a wound deep within me has been triggered.

Let's consider our above scenarios with this in mind.

Scenario One: In our first scenario we might hypothesise that a deeply ingrained abandonment wound from our early childhood has been triggered by this row with our partner. Our inner child is terrified. Being in this situation with our partner is really scary and uncertain. It feels too much for us to bear, so we do all we can to fix it, apologising as quickly as possible so that life can go back to feeling safe again and so that we can feel secure in our relationship with our partner. The thought of being abandoned by our partner is too much for us psychologically. This is a deeply distressing thing for us to experience, and one that we don't believe we can survive, so we do everything in our power to make life feel safe again.

Learning Note: A wound is an extremely difficult or traumatising experience (or set of experiences) that causes you intense pain. Similarly, an abandonment wound is an extremely difficult or traumatising experience (or set of experiences) that triggers emotional sensitivity to anything that feels like a rejection, for example feeling excluded, overlooked, misunderstood or that a relationship that is important to you is under threat.

Scenario Two: In this scenario we might hypothesise that deep down inside us our inner child has been triggered by seeing our friends out having fun together, and so feels excluded, something that is a very familiar feeling for us, for we have experienced it before, and it deeply wounded us when it occurred. As a child, feeling excluded can be incredibly impactful, especially because in our early years we have an egocentric view of the world, believing that everything that happens in our immediate environment is somehow linked to us. For this reason we do not have the understanding or awareness to not take things personally, and so we internalise what has happened, making it about us. In this scenario we might jump to conclusions, perhaps thinking, 'They planned this without me, they don't care about me the way I thought they did.' We might even internalise our anger and make this about us, 'I always knew I was boring company and that my friends thought so too. Why do I bother making an effort with them? I'm so stupid and naive.' The logical adult self, if he or she were in control, might consider alternative reasons our friends were out together without us, but when our inner child has been triggered our logical adult self often goes off line, and so too do our rational thoughts. This can result in deep pain and suffering for both our inner child and our adult self, especially when we feel left out, unloved or rejected (and these feelings echo our early ones).

Scenario Three: In our final scenario we might hypothesise that our inner child has time and again deeply questioned our standing and belonging in our relationships. So much so that when our best friend forgets our birthday this deep inner wound and questioning is triggered almost immediately and we regress to the scared little child inside us who has always felt extremely uncertain and unsure whether we can relax into our relationships and trust that we are safe and secure in them. With this regression we are likely feeling uncertain again, like the little child within us who more than anything wants to trust that somebody loves us and won't abandon us, and that we are worthy of this love and security, but that feels too scared and too wary to believe this. Especially given our best friend, who we thought loved us and was of safe standing in our life, has just let us down hugely (remember here that when our inner child is triggered we are responding from a place of believing everything that is happening around us is somehow linked to us). We might also hypothesise here that this experience with our best friend has resurfaced memories from an early relationship in our life where someone we loved deeply didn't offer us consistent and reliable love, and so our best friend forgetting our birthday feels deeply painful and familiar for us.

Learning Note: When our inner child becomes triggered we may respond in an extremely heightened way to the situation we find ourselves in. This response may feel extreme to others in the situation, and even to us when our logical adult self regains control. This is because we are responding from the deeply hurt little child we were when we originally went through the difficult or traumatising experience (or set of experiences) that led to this deep inner wound we still carry, an experience we have not yet healed from, and that continues to have an intense emotional hold over us.

CONNECTING WITH YOUR INNER CHILD

The wounded inner child is our bringer of healing ... one who makes whole.
CARL JUNG

When I guide clients through inner child work in my therapy room, I always begin in the same way. Let's pause to practise this together now.

HEALING EXERCISE

Pause to complete this exercise before continuing.

Read and complete each step in order, before moving on to read and complete the next step.

When I do this exercise, I close my eyes (opening them only to read the next step, before closing them again as I complete it), as this helps me to deeply connect to the experience.

Part One
Imagine a beautiful little child in front you. They are inconsolable. Hot salty tears are rolling down their little face and they look so lost and alone.

How do you feel towards this child?

Take a moment to consider this (there is no right or wrong here, so go with your instinct).

Part Two
Now imagine this beautiful little child is someone you know. Really bring them to life in your mind's eye. Their clothes. Their hair. The expression on their sad little face.

How do you feel towards them in this moment?

Part Three
Imagine this beautiful little child shifts so that they now become you. A much younger version of you. You recognise their clothing, the ways their hair is styled, the sad expression on their face. Drink them in, paying attention to how you feel in their presence.

How do you feel towards this little child in front of you?

Do you feel drawn to connect with them? If so, in what way?

If you would like to, connect with them in this way now.

Once you have completed this exercise, take some time to decompress. Inner child work can be deeply emotive. How does your inner child want to be supported in this moment? Perhaps he or she would like some fresh air or a soothing cup or tea. Perhaps he or she would like you to write down how you are feeling in order to release the emotions you have been carrying for a long time now. Listen to your inner child. Connect within. Your inner child has a message for you.

The first year after my father's death was a very dark one for me. I felt so alone and so heartbroken, yet life went on. The people I loved were of course there for me, but in that darkness I felt so disconnected and dazed. The world continued as if nothing had happened, and this broke my heart all over again. How could this be? How could the world go on in this way without him? On the surface I was thriving. I went back to supporting my clients, I returned to my lectures, I engaged in life with my boyfriend and friends, there physically but never fully present. However, beneath the surface I was falling apart. My anxiety was at an all-time high. Everything felt terrifying. Driving, socialising, even something as simple as going to the cinema with my boyfriend caused alarm bells to go off in my head and a panic attack to ensue. The world was no longer safe without the security of my father by my side, grounding me and supporting me as he had for so long, and this manifested for me as intense anxiety. My inner child was terrified and I was absolutely consumed by her fear.

REFLECTIVE PAUSE

Amidst this constant terror and fear I was surrounded by, what could I have done to care for and soothe my terrified inner child?

Pause here for a moment to consider this before reading on.

Let me take you on a journey to show you how to soothe your inner child.

HEALING EXERCISE

Practise this exercise in a safe space, free from distraction. Get cosy, grab your favourite blanket and relax into the chair or bed supporting your body. Settle in for a healing journey.

To begin, gently close down your eyes and connect your awareness to your breath, taking slow and steady deep breaths in and out. Fall into a rhythm that feels natural to you and as you tune in to your breath and the rise and fall of your chest, notice how your body is responding to this nurturing stillness. All you have to do in this moment is breathe. Everything else can wait. This is your time and if you notice your mind starting to drift off as we complete this exercise together, gently return your awareness to your breath and the rise and fall of your chest. If you would like an extra anchor in this moment, place one hand on your belly and the other on your heart, and connect with the gentle movement of your body.

I invite you now to visualise an image of your younger self. Allow this younger version of you to show up exactly as he or she is and at whatever age he or she arrives as. There is no right or wrong here. Your intuition and inner wisdom will guide you, so trust what surfaces. Really bring to mind this image of your younger self. What are you wearing? What way is your hair? What expression is on your little face? Connect with this younger version of you in your mind's eye as vividly as you can. Where is this younger version of you as you visualise this? What surrounds this little child who has come to mind? Trust whatever arises for you.

When the time feels right, visualise your adult self walking towards this little child to gently let them know you have arrived.

How do they respond? Do they welcome you or are they wary? Allow them to take the lead. Spend some time with them, perhaps slowly getting to know each other if they are cautious or offering them some love and affection if they are glad you have arrived. If they are happy for you to do so, and if it feels right for you, hold their hand, embrace them, cuddle them close. Notice how this feels in your body as you do this. Connect with them as deeply as feels right for you both.

Next let them know that you are here to take care of them and to look after them. Let them know that they are no longer alone. Ask them how they have been feeling. Allow them space to share all they are carrying, and when they are finished, comfort them and validate how they have been feeling and the weight they have been carrying. Remind them that they are no longer alone and that you have arrived to care for them and to look after them. Soothe them exactly as you would a small child, reassuring them that whatever happens you will be there with them and that you will look after them and keep them safe. Spend as much time soothing and comforting them as they need ... as you both need.

When you are both ready, let them know that it is time for you to leave, but share with them that you can tuck them up snugly in your heart so that they can stay with you if this is what they want. If this is what they desire, visualise gently tucking them into a big cosy bed inside your heart until they feel comfortable, safe and snug. Share with them that you know how incredibly exhausted they are from constantly being on high alert so that they can keep you safe. Thank them for this, for how hard they have been working to look after and protect you. However, let them know that it's time for them to rest now, safe in the knowledge that you are here and that as an adult you can look after you both. Let them know that it's your job to do this now, so they can rest. Reassure them of this and do what you can to help them to relax, perhaps rubbing their hair, reading them a story or singing them a song, or sitting with them for as long as they need before their eyes begin to close. Remind them that they are safe and that just as has happened today, whenever they need you, you will be close by to comfort and soothe them, especially if they feel scared. Stay with them until you feel ready to return to the outside world, and when this time comes, gently retreat, leaving them to rest.

When you feel it is time to finish this exercise and return to the space you are in, slowly start to shift your awareness back to the outer world. Begin by gently wiggling your fingers and toes and then slowly stretch your body, perhaps raising your arms above your head, bringing your shoulders to meet your ears, and then pulling your shoulder blades together behind you. Move your body in whatever way you need to and when you feel ready, slowly open your eyes, coming back into the environment you are in. Now check in with how you are feeling. Are you feeling relaxed, comforted and soothed? I really hope so. Remember that you can return to this exercise anytime you need to: if you can soothe your scared inner child, you will in turn also soothe yourself.

This powerful exercise is one I use regularly with my clients, and one they go on to practise outside our sessions. This is one I too use when feeling emotional, scared, angry or sad, and one I wish I had known about in that dark year after my father's death. I really hope this deeply healing exercise is as powerful for you and that you choose to practise it, returning to it as often as you need it. If there is one lesson inner child work has taught me, it is that no one else can soothe us in the way that we can soothe, love and care for ourselves, so hold yourself until your pain has subsided. Everything is going to be okay.

As I sit here thinking back to that incredibly dark year that followed my father's death, what is catching me by surprise is the realisation of why I reacted to his death and to losing him in the way I did. At the age of 25 I was an adult, a young adult, yes, but an adult nonetheless; yet my father's death absolutely crippled me. I was surrounded by support in that first dark year yet felt so alone; alone and absolutely consumed by anxiety. You see, my father's death felt like an abandonment to me and one that completely paralysed me. However, this was not my first abandonment, and not the first time I had felt so alone and so terrified. Deep within my 25-year-old adult self, my inner child was responding from the original abandonment wound I carried deep inside. Because, as a newborn baby, I was separated from my safety, my security and the only person I had ever known; I was placed for adoption on my arrival into the world.

When I picture my own newborn daughters on their arrival into the world, I visualise the tiny, helpless, stunned little creatures they were. I picture how heavily they relied on me and my body that was so familiar to them; the smell, the comfort, the safety in proximity. As I sit here I wonder what it would have been like for them to have been separated from me. I wonder too what it was like for me to have been separated from my comfort and safety as a newborn baby, so tiny, helpless and stunned. I don't consciously remember this separation, but what I do remember is the huge impact it has had on my entire life.

ATTACHMENT TRAUMA

Learning Note: Attachment is something that is widely spoken about in connection with the psychology of how we function in our relationships. In simple terms, attachment is our relationship or bond with our caregivers or parents in our early childhood. This bond is the premise for all other relationships in our life, and if we felt that our caregivers responded reliably and consistently to our needs in our early childhood, typically we go on to feel 'secure' in our other relationships, believing that it is generally safe to trust our loved ones and friends. If, however, we grew up feeling that we received inconsistent or unreliable connection from our caregivers this may cause us to feel 'insecure' in our relationships and in the wider world, and so we may find it hard to trust that others will reliably meet our needs and we may question our standing in their lives, and indeed in the world.

Years of therapy have helped me to grow awareness to the little girl deep within me who has always felt scared and unsure. This little girl has always watched from the sidelines, wary of those around her because at times, even with her daddy's safe presence in her life, things felt scary and uncertain. When I close my eyes to picture her now, allowing whatever image that's there to come, she arrives in my mind's eye as a tiny newborn baby. Screaming and thrashing, inconsolable because she's alone. Alone and scared. Alone and uncertain. What is happening? Where have her home and safety from the past nine months gone? Does nobody love her? Can nobody hear her cries? Does nobody love me? Can nobody hear my cries?

The attachment wound I experienced as a newborn baby led me and my inner child to believe that life was unsafe and that I could never rely on anyone not to abandon me, as was my experience right from day one. I have carried this wound deep inside me throughout my life, and so growing up I was very sensitive in my relationships. Could I rely on these people in my life? Could I trust them? This wariness and deeply embedded fear led me to believe I had to constantly protect myself and so I never fully gave myself to others. Why? Because I never again wanted to feel the pain I experienced when I felt abandoned that first time, the pain that surfaced again when my father died, crippling me and causing the world to feel too unsafe to psychologically bear.

I share my attachment trauma and deep inner wound with you so that you can consider if you too are carrying a deep inner wound that has stayed with you your entire life, and that from time to time, even now, can get triggered. Does your inner child respond to this wound, like mine does, becoming very emotional when this happens? Does your inner child work hard to protect you? If so I imagine they feel exhausted from all this hard work. Do they crave rest, as in the healing exercise above?

REFLECTIVE PAUSE

Take some time to consider the above questions. Write down whatever comes to mind. Allow yourself time and space to grow your awareness and to work through and release some of the emotions you have been carrying for a very long time. This is how to heal. This is powerful work. Give yourself this gift.

Learning Note: In the above paragraphs I speak about our inner child working hard to protect us from experiencing hurt or pain like the hurt and pain we once experienced when our original wounds were created. In these moments our inner child will be triggered by something they are sensitive to, and so will quickly come to the surface to do all they can to keep us safe. For example, as my inner child is so sensitive to abandonment, she may rise to the surface if she feels let down by someone and fearful they may reject me or cause me pain. This may influence me to make decisions or to behave in ways I wouldn't if my logical adult self were in control. For example, my inner child may trigger me to run away from a situation or person, or to create a barrier to keep them at arm's length. Similarly she may prompt me to become defensive or to avoid something or someone, or to try to control a situation so that life feels safer. Typically our inner child will present at the age they were when the original wound occurred. For example, my inner child often presents as a newborn baby because of the attachment wound I experienced at birth.

REFLECTIVE PAUSE

What does your inner child try to protect you from? How does he or she show up when this is triggered within you and how does it impact your behaviour? Consider too what age/s your inner child shows up as and why they are stuck at these ages.

Consider using my above questions as journal prompts. Building this awareness is incredibly helpful. This is the work. This is how to heal your inner child.

HEALING THE WOUNDS YOUR INNER CHILD IS CARRYING

To take care of ourselves we must go back to take care of the wounded child inside us.
THICH NHAT HANH

> *When I was working to soothe my distressed inner child and to heal from my attachment trauma, I wrote:*

- *Therapeutic letters – just for my eyes, and my therapist's, if it felt safe to show her. These were letters I would never send; they were letters to help me understand, work through and release the emotional pain and distress my inner child was carrying deep inside.*

- *Therapeutic stories to activate my inner child and to see where she – or my subconscious – would lead me. Stories that began with sentences such as:*

    – 'Once upon a time there lived a princess in a beautiful castle …'

    – 'Deep down the little girl inside me …';

    – 'There once was a beautiful little girl who loved to …'

    – 'Once upon a time a little girl went on an adventure …'

- *Random paragraphs or 'brain dumps' – whatever was filling my mind. These paragraphs were mainly emotional in nature, expressing my anger or sadness. I allowed myself to write whatever came to me and sometimes my emotions were so intense my pen would puncture the page and my writing would become a scrawl. On those occasions I welcomed this as part of the process, trusting my inner knowing was guiding me on my healing journey.*

During this period I also expressed myself and the insecure little girl inside me by drawing and painting pictures. An artist I am not, and for the most part these drawings mirrored those my seven-year-old daughter proudly carries home from school, but this process was one that was deeply healing for me.

Perhaps it would be deeply healing for you too.

HEALING EXERCISE

In a safe space free from interruptions, sit down and write, just as I did.

Do so with no expectations of yourself, and allow whatever arises to flow as you put pen to paper, connecting inwards to that deep inner knowing you have always carried inside.

Part One
Write a letter from your wounded inner child to your adult self.

Allow them space and time to share what they have been carrying.

Allow them space and time to express their emotions and all their struggles.

Allow them space and time to grieve and to mourn; to express their anger and disappointment;

to share their truth and to show up exactly as they want to.

There are no right or wrongs here. Your inner child knows what he or she needs to say.

Part Two
When you feel ready, whether that's immediately or after taking some time and space to process what has arisen for you in Part One, write a letter replying to your inner child. In your letter shower your younger self with love, care, compassion, understanding and validation. Offer them everything you wish you had received on those occasions that you didn't.

Once you have completed this exercise, give yourself some time to ground and centre yourself. Lovingly care for yourself in whatever way you need to. This work is hard, so care for yourself as you continue on your deep healing journey.

REPARENTING YOUR INNER CHILD
By reparenting our Inner Child, we can release and heal the pain from the past.
MARGARET PAUL

When my trauma wound is activated or triggered now, and my inner child takes the reins, I gently and compassionately offer love, comfort and reassurance to the scared little girl inside me (either in our healing visualisation exercise above, or through a healing letter that I write to her, or from her). I listen to my inner child. I validate her. I tell her it's okay to feel the way she does. I lovingly soothe her (and in turn my adult self) through practising the somatic techniques we learned in Step Three (perhaps today would be a nice time to revisit these techniques to remind yourself of their power) and through showering her with compassion (as we will learn in Step Six). This process is often referred to as the reparenting process, the goal being to provide your inner child with what they feel they lacked or didn't receive during childhood.

> **REFLECTIVE PAUSE**
>
> Spend a moment considering how an attentive caring parent responds to their distressed or angry child when he or she is activated. Pause here to consider this before reading on.
>
> Now I invite you to imagine you are in the supermarket walking from aisle to aisle, placing items in your basket as you go. Suddenly you come across a mother and daughter. The little girl

is screaming through tears, and as you watch her distress you notice she has a newly formed bump on her forehead.

How do you imagine this little girl's mother is responding to her? Pause here to consider this question, being open to whatever arrives.

When we consider how an attentive, caring parent responds to their distressed child, we may imagine that they will shower them with love and affection, mirroring their pain and acknowledging the distress the child is experiencing, for example 'You're so angry you fell and hurt yourself, my poor little baby, let me rub your forehead to take away the pain.' Not only will this be very validating for the child, it will also model to them how to identify and express their emotions, and that emotional expression is welcome and allowed.

When considering how to reparent your inner child, hold the above in mind. Consider too questions such as:

- What is my inner child yearning for?

- How can I comfort and soothe my inner child?

- What did I lack while growing up? How can I provide this to my inner child now?

- What is my inner child carrying that it is now time for them to put down?

- How is my inner child trying to protect me? What are they doing to ensure this?

HEALING EXERCISE

Take out your journal and pen, and spend some time answering the above questions and considering how you can start to reparent the little boy or girl you carry deep inside.

Perhaps there is something you can do when you have finished this journal exercise to begin this journey.

Give yourself this gift. Your inner child will thank you for it.

STEP FOUR HEAL YOUR INNER CHILD SUMMARY

Throughout our journey in Step Four Heal your Inner Child we have connected on many levels with these younger versions of us we carry deep inside. We have allowed the younger versions of us to surface and we have lovingly considered their needs and how our adult selves can honour them. We have learned to soothe and comfort our inner child when they are distressed, we have visualised them, we have heard from them, we have written to them and we have begun reparenting them to offer them everything they yearned for when they were most in need. Now that you have started this deeply healing journey with your inner child, I invite you to continue it, keeping your inner child close and listening to them when they call on you. Connect with them daily. Soothe them. Nurture them. Make space for them. Continue offering them the love and care you have shown them throughout our healing journey. I really hope connecting with your inner child is as powerful for you as it is for me, and that you continue to practise this inner child healing, returning to it as often as you need to. If there is one lesson inner child work has taught me, it is that no one else can soothe us in the way we can soothe, love and care for ourselves, so hold yourself until your pain has subsided. Everything is going to be okay.

STEP FIVE

SILENCE YOUR INNER CRITIC

*Because beating yourself up
gives you nothing but bruises.*

Imagine this: you're at home preparing to leave the house. You're dressed in smart clothes, your bag is ready at the door, you've eaten and taken care of all of the necessities, when all of a sudden you spill the last dregs of your coffee all over yourself! You rush around trying to tidy yourself up, knowing that this mishap is costing you precious time you don't have.

Question: What thoughts are running through your head?

Pause here to consider this for a moment before reading on.

If I were to guess, I imagine there are two scenarios that could possibly be going on for you:

Scenario One: You're soothing yourself: 'It's okay, work/the party/Julie will wait. This happens to the best of us, I'll quickly clean myself up and get going.'

Scenario Two: You are criticising yourself as if you've made a massive mistake: 'You idiot, how could you be so clumsy? You're worse than a child, you're going to be late now and you've nobody to blame but yourself. What the hell are you going to wear now? Everything else is dirty because you are too bloody lazy to put on a wash and sort your life out. You're going to look terrible and everyone is going to notice you're the last to arrive. Serves you right.'

Now I'm not a betting woman, but if I were, I would bet my bottom dollar that Scenario Two is closest to the one you imagined playing out for you… am I right? If so, continue reading: Step Five Silence your Inner Critic is for you.

DOES YOUR INTERNAL VOICE GUIDE YOU OR BEGUILE YOU?

Inside all of us lies an inner voice that guides us. On some days this voice can be quietly confident and encouraging: 'You've got this'. On other days, it can be cautious and protective: 'Is this the right thing for you? Perhaps you need some time to consider it before taking the leap.' Sometimes this voice can be assertive and determined: 'This is your path and now is your time!' However, on *many* days this voice can be hugely self-critical and judgemental: 'You're a disaster. Why can you never do the things you say you will?'; 'You look terrible. Look at everyone around you, you don't compare'; 'Did you really just say that? Stop talking so much, it's embarrassing.'

For as long as I can remember my inner critic has been LOUD. Not only loud but ever-present and mean as hell. She'd boss me around and tell me that I was boring, with nothing of interest to contribute. Not just that, she'd tell me I was the odd one out who didn't belong; I was fat, my skin was too pale and I was ugly; and that I would never amount to anything in life. Alongside this horrible behaviour, she'd rarely stand up for me or encourage or motivate me; rather, she'd berate me and pick me apart, so that I was left feeling underserving, unworthy and unlovable. And when it came to guidance? It was like she was guiding me to stay in the shadows and play small. God forbid I ever try to put myself out there or take a leap of faith, oh no, my inner critic was having none of that!

For years my inner critic ruled me and treated me so unkindly. In fact as I sit here thinking back to the power and influence she had over me, it makes me so sad to consider the huge impact she has had on my life and the countless times she has held me back in all aspects of my journey, from personal to professional; from romantic relationships to friendships; from childhood to motherhood. All due to the narrative she created about me and the world around me.

Sadly our inner critic is something we all have in common, no matter what stage of our healing journey we are on. For many, he or she can be as loud, mean and ever-present as mine always was; for others, after some tender loving care and challenge, their internal critic can be present less frequently and can be softer. However, I'll be honest, I have yet to meet anyone who is living completely free of that voice. Have you? (This is not to say that I don't believe we can hugely change the relationship we hold with our inner critic, because this I absolutely do believe. But I'm getting ahead of myself!)

REFLECTIVE EXERCISE

Spend a moment considering how your inner voice showed up for you throughout your life. Was it there to guide you and encourage you, or to berate, judge and criticise you? Write down whatever comes to mind, trusting that the words that need to arrive will come. Allow yourself time and space to really reflect on this and to carve out the relationship you have had with your inner voice over the years. There are no right or wrongs here, only learnings.

THE DEVELOPMENT OF OUR INNER CRITIC

The constellation of our fears manifests as the Inner Critic. This psychological construct can trick us into believing the very worst about ourselves and our ability to create or do anything of value in the world.
DENISE JACOBS

Our inner critic develops from external voices we experience throughout our lives, particularly throughout our early childhood. Perhaps it was messaging you received from your parents or caregivers:

- 'That's not good enough, you're so lazy, you need to work harder.'

- 'You're far too loud. Quieten down, for God's sake.'

- 'Look at your sister, she's such a smart girl. Why can't you be more like her?'

- 'That top really doesn't suit you, it makes your arms look so big. Go and change before we leave the house.'

Maybe it was comments you heard from a teacher in school that you internalised without even realising you were doing so:

- 'Maths really isn't your forte is it, you stupid boy?'

- 'You are such a shy little thing, you wouldn't say boo to a goose, but you need to stand up for yourself more or people will walk all over you.'

- 'Don't you have a big appetite? And such big bones!'

- 'You'll never amount to anything if you continue on like that.'

Friends and acquaintances may have also left their mark on you:

- 'You're so boring, I'm not playing with you any more.'
- 'No one wants to sit beside you, you've no friends.'
- 'Your tummy looks funny, do you have a baby in there?'
- 'Shut up, no one wants to listen to you.'

Or someone who has caused you great hurt in the past:

- 'Nobody loves you or cares about you.'
- 'You should be grateful I'm even paying you attention.'
- 'You are worthless and don't forget it.'
- 'Stop crying, you're pathetic.'

And when it comes to the media, how could we ever escape the harmful impact of the narrative that is both explicitly and implicitly broadcast to us?

Conversely, our inner critic can also stem from the stories we create for ourselves, about ourselves. Take me for example, being placed for adoption as a newborn baby hugely impacted the way I viewed myself and the worth I had to offer the world. It was like I created this story very early on in my life that due to being given away as a baby I was unwanted and worthless. Sad as it is to admit, it was as if I created this narrative within me that queried what a person who wasn't even wanted by her own mother had to offer in life. This was a *core belief* I held for many years and one my inner voice knew was a weakness for me, so chose to return to time and again. Due to her constant beratement, my inner critic led me to believe I wasn't good enough; as a daughter, friend, partner, psychologist, mother, even person.

Learning Note: A core belief is a foundational idea or belief we hold about ourselves or the world around us. These can be universal; for example, most people hold the core belief that it is wrong to steal or to be unfaithful when in a committed relationship. Core beliefs can also be specific to the way we were brought up, in that we may learn in our families of origin not to speak about private matters outside the family home or that we protect or are loyal to family members at all costs. We can also develop and hold core beliefs that relate to our standing in the world, like the core belief I held that I had nothing to offer those around me. Often these core beliefs can be negative, such as mine was, and these negative core beliefs can really impact our lives and cause us to self-sabotage.

Examples of negative core beliefs include:

- 'I will never amount to anything – I'm too stupid.'

- 'I cannot trust anyone. People always eventually let me down.'

- 'I am unlovable.'

Negative core beliefs can also cause us to hold ourselves back in life. For example, if you are constantly telling yourself that you'll amount to nothing, how likely is it that you'll ever take the risk and try? Rather you'll hinder your success by inaction, self-sabotage or by taking actions that will negatively impact your trajectory.

I once worked with a woman named Anna who was in her 30s and living a very fulfilling life. She had a home she loved, a job she enjoyed, friends she had known from childhood and a supportive family. Anna was happy in all aspects of her life, except in her love life. She had dated over the years but had never had a significant relationship, and although her biggest wish in life was to meet a partner, and in time, become a mother, Anna wasn't having much luck when it came to dating.

Anna and I explored the 'whys' of this during numerous therapy sessions until one day, during a particularly emotive inner child visualisation, Anna realised that deep down she was afraid to let someone into her life because of her very early relationship with her maternal grandmother, who continuously rejected her, bad-mouthed her and compared her to her mother as a child. Because of this, Anna held the core belief that she was unworthy and undeserving of love. This belief, although one she wasn't consciously aware of for most of her life (even though it was deeply ingrained in her), due to her grandmother passing away when she was very young, was causing her to sabotage every possibility of a relationship before it even began. This, coupled with a fear that having a partner might negatively impact her ability to achieve in life, due to her focus no longer being solely on her career, meant that Anna was subconsciously writing off potential partners with any excuse she could think of and keeping people at arm's length. In fact, it was only when she realised how much power this core belief held over her that she was able to 'feel the fear and do it anyway' and very gently open herself up to love.

About a year after our work together concluded, I received an email from Anna with a lovely photo of her partner and newborn baby, thanking me for helping her along her journey. It is at moments like these I feel so privileged to work in the role that I do.

REFLECTIVE EXERCISE

Reach for a pen and paper and list three core beliefs you hold about the world and three core beliefs you hold about yourself.

Of the three you hold about yourself, rate them from 1 to 5, with 1 being the belief that is most ingrained in you.

Spend a few moments considering these core beliefs and where you may have developed them from. Whose voices did you internalise in creating them and in the development of your inner voice?

Finally, reflect on whether you still wholeheartedly believe these points to be true, or whether there may be some scope within you to challenge them now, particularly if they are negative. Spend some time with this, as it may be a particularly healing exercise for you. No matter where you are on your journey, remember that this is the work, and how brave you are to be pursuing it.

THE FUNCTION OF OUR INNER CRITIC

The Inner Critic is a source of shame. It finds every aspect of the natural 'you' unsatisfactory, and it is relentlessly trying to change everything. There is no part of you that can avoid its piercing gaze – even the depths of your feelings, dreams, and impulses that you might be able to hide from the outside world.
HAL STONE

When I consider my inner critic with compassion and curiosity (which can sometimes be extremely hard because she can be so harsh!) I realise that deep down she is trying to protect me from pain I once experienced. For example, when she tells me how unlovable I am, she does so to encourage me to keep my distance from people so they cannot cause me the hurt and pain I experienced in my early years when placed for adoption. It is like my inner critic vividly remembers this pain and how much it paralysed me, so cautions me (albeit in an incredibly berating way) to keep my distance and to not expect love and care from others. She knows that this love and care, despite how earnestly it is desired, isn't always available. Realising this was such a learning for me and caused me to view my inner critic very differently. Yes, she can still be as mean and bossy as ever, but with this newfound understanding her harsh remarks don't seem quite as cutting.

All our behaviours have a function. For example, rumination can help us to feel we are preventing ourselves from making the same mistake again, while engaging in anxious thinking can help us to feel we have control of the future so nothing unexpected can hit us. Our inner critic, this nasty voice inside our head, can serve a purpose too. This function can differ from person to person, but engaging in critical self-talk can lead us to believe many things, for example that we are bettering ourselves, conforming with society, or preventing ourselves from making a fool of ourselves. Our critical inner voice can also feel like a protector or a tough-love teacher, and we can even believe that it is keeping us safe from harm and helping us to reach the incredibly high (often unrealistic) standards we set for ourselves.

These functions are typically formed during our early childhood when we internalise external voices and believe other people's views of us and the world. For this reason, these functions can often be very simplistic and rigid and if we were able to assess and recalibrate them, as I describe above, perhaps they could be more helpful for us as we navigate life. However, this is something that rarely happens because so often our inner critic is both deeply ingrained in us and entirely subconscious.

Because our inner critic typically forms when we are very young, often the function it has no longer serves us as adults. Rather, it can hold us back in life, keeping us playing small; not to mention the hugely significant impact our inner critic can have on our self-belief and self-worth. With this in mind, it is so important to quieten this inner criticism and judgement, and as luck would have it, you can read on below to receive a step-by-step guide on how exactly to do just that.

QUIETENING YOUR INNER CRITIC

Your inner critic is simply a part of you that needs more self love.
AMY LEIGH MERCREE

A huge part of the work I do in my therapy room is helping clients to quieten the constant barrage of judgement and self-criticism they experience in their mind. Sadly, this judgement and criticism is often so ingrained in us that we don't even notice its presence until, thanks to you finding yourself here, that suddenly begins to change.

REFLECTIVE EXERCISE

Taking today as an example, can you list five critical or judgemental things you've said to yourself?

Take a moment to consider this and list on paper the examples that come to mind.

My bet is that if you delve deep enough the criticism will be there ... am I right?

Speaking to ourselves in this way can feel so familiar because it's constant. Take the examples that just came to mind for you: would you ever say these words to someone you hold dear in your life? My guess is no, that you would be horrified at the idea. However, I imagine that these criticisms don't seem particularly harsh when you consider them as things you regularly say to yourself.

Why? Because sadly they are familiar. Constant. Deeply ingrained.

So how do you make meaningful change?

Because you so deserve to.

You so deserve to nurture yourself with love, understanding and kindness in the same way you do for those you adore most in the world.

Read that again.

STAGE ONE: BUILDING AWARENESS OF YOUR INNER CRITIC

Awareness is half the process. Without it change is impossible.

Building awareness of your inner critic is *paramount*. This begins with bringing your inner voice to the forefront of your mind. Every time he or she pipes up in a negative way, I urge you to take notice. With each challenge or judgement he or she passes I want you to register exactly what has been said in its entirety. It's time to bring to the fore that familiar occurrence that you so often barely take heed of (consciously, that is — because deep down, even if it doesn't register, it's hurting you enormously), due to the frequency with which you experience it, and to begin to change your relationship with it.

HEALING EXERCISE

Part A
Over the next 24 hours, carry with you a pen and pocket notebook and write down every *single* negative comment your inner critic fires at you.

Examples might include:

'Ugh, look at your skin.'

'You look fat in this; take it off.'

'You should have replied before now, what is wrong with you?'

'That's a big portion of dinner, isn't it?'

'Stop being so lazy.'

'You idiot.'

'Why do you always mess up? You are so stupid.'

'You are the worst mother/father/partner in the world.'

'Stop shouting.'

'You should have tried harder.'

'This house is a mess.'

'Don't bother even trying; you always fail.'

(Do any of the above sound familiar?)

Be ruthless (just as your inner critic is) in registering and recording these occurrences, and don't be tempted to just document them in your mind or in the notes app on your phone. There is power in writing and in the process, so I ask you to trust me and to carry out this healing exercise with intention and commitment. It's one I prescribe to my clients all the time, and a very powerful one at that. So go forth, take heed, and write!

This may be a very confronting exercise to complete, so be gentle with yourself. This is the work and my promise to you is that it will benefit you hugely. Trust the process and mind yourself as you go. This could be truly life-changing for you in the best way possible. You've got this.

Once you have finished this exercise, save these notes for later as we'll be returning to them.

Part B
In a safe and comfortable space, when you have time to do so, I encourage you take time to read the words you have written over the past 24 hours.

How does reading these words make you feel?

How do they register when you consider them in this way?

Are you surprised by anything you have written down or the frequency of the criticism and judgement that you've captured?

Is there anything in the information you've gathered that you would ever say to a loved one? If your answer is 'No', spend a moment reflecting on why you wouldn't say this to anyone else in your life but why you are in the habit of speaking to yourself in this way.

Note: Having a pen and paper to hand while doing Part B of this exercise will enhance your ability to reflect on this healing exercise. As beneficial as this work is, it can be painful and confronting, so be gentle with yourself as you complete this task.

Although you might not suspect this, building awareness of your inner critic will happen very quickly once you commit to it. In fact these three steps I'm outlining are truly transformational and you will see that very clearly during the process. For things to change, it is really important you do the work, so complete the above exercise to the best of your ability, and reap the rewards that will come as this powerful awareness becomes an everyday healing occurrence.

STAGE TWO: CATCHING YOUR INNER CRITIC AND STOPPING THEM IN THEIR TRACKS

The effort you put into this process will be truly transformational.

Once you've started building awareness of how frequently your inner critic appears and of just how harsh and judgemental they can be, it's time to begin catching them *every single time* they appear. Initially this will be hard to do. You have been living with your inner critic for countless years, so creating a new relationship with that internal voice inside your mind will take work and commitment. However, if the willingness is there, what I can promise you is that the effort you put into this process will be truly transformational. Imagine reducing the judgements you make about yourself every day even by half? Wouldn't that have a hugely significant impact on you? And we are aiming for far more than half!

With this in mind, each and every time your inner critic makes an appearance, register their occurrence – as in Stage One – and as you catch them, STOP THEM.

This 'stopping' process can take on a number of forms, which I outline below. My advice is to play around with them and try them on for size to see which feel like the best fit(s) for you. One size doesn't fit all, so the aim is to tailor-make a plan just for you.

Option One: Once you have caught your inner critic in action, answer them back!

This could take the form of replying to their latest quibble with an affirmation such as, 'I will not allow anyone to bully me, including you' or a retort like, 'I no longer want to hear your opinion, thank you very much!'

Choose your response and repeat it every time your inner critic judges or criticises you. You'll be surprised by how quickly this technique to catch and pause your inner in his or her tracks becomes a habit and how easy it will be to move on from this criticism in a way that feels very different for you.

Option Two: Every time your inner critic makes an appearance, take five deep breaths.

This interrupts and re-programmes the pattern that tends to play out every time your inner critic arrives. For example, instead of criticising yourself and allowing this to spiral out of control so that you instantly feel bad about yourself, pause and take five deep breaths. Not only will this interrupt and change the pattern, building a new, healthier one, it will also signal to your nervous system that you are safe, which will send a relaxation cue to your body.

Option Three: Repeat a positive, loving affirmation each and every time your inner critic appears.

Positive affirmations are scientifically proven to build new neural pathways in our brains. This means that these processes and practices become easier and more automatic with practice and repetition. Positive affirmations strengthen our positive thinking and optimism, reducing rumination and negative spiralling and building a more positive perception of ourselves.

Some possible positive affirmations to repeat to yourself are:

- 'I am enough, I have enough, I do enough.'
- 'I love and accept myself exactly as I am.'
- 'I am calm and nobody can disturb my peace.'
- 'I have the power to focus on the positives.'
- 'I am at peace in my body and in my life.'
- 'I am joyfully creating a new habit with my inner voice.'
- 'I deserve love, especially from myself.'

Option Four: When your inner critic arrives, use your senses to mindfully ground you.

One of the most powerful ways of coming back to the present moment, especially when you are up in your head and disconnected from your body, is to use your senses to ground you to the here and now. So next time (and every time!) your inner critic arrives on the scene, use your sight to locate the most beautiful object in your vicinity (e.g. a flower or a painting); your hearing to tune into a sound that you can pinpoint (e.g. birds singing or a song that's playing on the radio); your sense of touch to feel the texture of an item within your reach (e.g. the warmth of a mug in your hand or the coolness of a glass of water); your sense of smell to breathe in a beautiful aroma (e.g. freshly cut grass or your perfume or aftershave); and your sense of taste to become fully aware of something you are eating or a flavour lingering in your mouth.

This process interrupts the pattern of how you typically respond to your inner critic and redirects you to a more healthy (and helpful!) response.

Option Five: Befriend your inner critic every time they invite themselves in.

As we've discussed, our inner critic typically serves a purpose, but because it likely formed when we were very young it has long outgrown its usefulness.

Pause here to complete this reflective exercise before reading on.

REFLECTIVE EXERCISE

Imagine a little boy or a little girl. They stand in front of you having made a simple mistake, such as spilling a glass of water or knocking over a book.

Spend a moment considering whether you think a beneficial way for them to learn how to not make this mistake again would be to shout at them: 'You idiot! You are so stupid. You weren't watching what you were doing and now you've ruined everything! You are so worthless and such a waste of space.'

I don't imagine you would do this, would you? In fact, I imagine speaking to them in this way would cause them to feel a sense of great shame, inferiority and perhaps even fear . . . Just as our inner critic can lead us to feel.

With this in mind, when your inner critic invites themselves in, I welcome you to befriend them by catching their arrival and conversing with them. For example, you might say something like, 'I know you are trying to keep me safe and protect me from getting hurt, but as an adult I am capable of taking risks and making decisions for myself, and when you criticise and judge me it knocks my confidence. Instead, could you please offer some empathy and encouragement?'

This is a great way to catch and stop the inner judgement and criticism your inner critic fires at you. Once you start this practice you will be surprised at how quickly speaking to your inner critic in this way becomes a habit for you and of how healing it can be.

As you play around with the above suggestions, pay attention to which options work best for you in your endeavour to CATCH and STOP your inner critic and their barrage of judgements and criticisms. Remember, the aim here is to tailor a plan just for you. Good luck, and remember, the way to make a change here is to practise, practise, practise!

STAGE THREE: MEETING YOUR INNER CRITIC WITH SELF-COMPASSION

If you were able to meet yourself moment to moment with compassion, everything would change.

The third and final step in silencing your inner critic may be the most challenging step of all because it will likely feel the most foreign to you. In Step Three, every time your inner critic arrives, you are going to meet it with kindness, understanding and encouragement. We will dive deeply into compassion in Step Six Cultivate Compassion, but for now, just be aware that self-compassion is exactly that – showering yourself with kindness, understanding and encouragement, and quietening the judgement and criticism that can be so automatic for us.

Bringing self-compassion into my life changed it completely. I had always known what the concept meant but I never truly put it into practice until I began working with a therapist called Bríd, when I was pregnant with my second daughter. Bríd was a no-nonsense lady in her 60s who could see immediately that I was yearning to be mothered in our sessions. Not only that, but Bríd could also see that I was desperately craving empathy, love and warmth, and that the little girl inside me was so tired from always being on high alert and in protect mode. Bríd, being an incredibly skilled therapist, could see that the person I most needed this empathy, love and warmth from was me.

Bríd made me aware of this very early in our work together and I resented her for it! Why couldn't she just give me what I was desperately yearning for? Why was she making me work so hard to do this for myself? Wasn't the entire point of therapy to have someone there to hold my hand as I navigated these painful and uncharted waters?

However, during our time together, what Bríd gave me was so much more than I was craving from her. She gave me the gift of self-compassion.

With every single hurt I raised, she helped me to meet it with self-compassion. With every single wound I licked, she helped me to meet it with self-compassion. With every single grudge I recounted, she helped me to meet it with self-compassion. And boy, was that powerful.

My compassion-focused therapy with Bríd was also incredibly powerful in reducing my shame, self-criticism and judgement. I spoke to Bríd about so many things I felt deeply ashamed of. Things I would never dare to say aloud to another human being. Yet Bríd helped me to normalise all the emotions I was experiencing and to see how human they were. Was I the terribly flawed human being I once firmly believed I was, or was I really just a normal human being with normal emotions, reactions and painful memories? This realisation was life-changing for me. The work transformed my life completely and I owe that to Bríd and the wonderful (but incredibly hard) work we completed together that year.

It is now time for me to pass this gift to you, dear reader. Do with it what you will, but if there is one thing that you can offer yourself today, this week, this month, it's self-compassion. It changed my life and it can change yours too.

Self-compassion has three main components:

1. Offering the same kindness, understanding and compassion to ourselves as we so easily and freely give to those around us (rather than self-judgement, criticism and harshness).

2. Recognising our shared humanity and connection to others, in the sense that none of us are perfect; we are all mere human beings who struggle, make mistakes, and carry vulnerabilities and imperfections.

3. Taking a mindful approach to our struggles and recognising and leaning into the experience we are going through and how we can accept this struggle and support ourselves and our needs through it.

Not only does it help to lower self-judgement and self-criticism, self-compassion has also been found to reduce anxiety, depression and stress; increase optimism and overall wellbeing; and act as a buffer against distressing experiences such as trauma.

> **REFLECTIVE EXERCISE**
>
> Grab a pen and paper and spend a moment imagining how you would likely be feeling in this moment with coffee dripping all over you, the is clock ticking and your inner critic out in full force. Write what comes to mind without putting too much pressure on yourself. Trust that your inner wisdom will guide you.
>
> ***Pause here to complete this exercise before continuing to read.***

Let's revisit our coffee story which you may remember from the beginning of this chapter:

You're at home preparing to leave the house. You're dressed in smart clothes, your bag is ready at the door, you've eaten and taken care of all of the necessities, when all of a sudden you spill the last dregs of your coffee all over yourself! You rush around trying to tidy yourself up, knowing that this mishap is costing you precious time you don't have.

Now, when we originally visited this scenario, I postulated that in this moment, with coffee spilled all down your front, you are very likely berating and criticising yourself: 'You idiot, how could you be so clumsy? You're worse than a child. You're going to be late now and you've nobody to blame but yourself.'

If you are anything like me, in the above scenario you would be running around like a headless chicken, bumping into things, knocking things over, and causing unnecessary chaos, feeling flustered and in full-blown stress mode. Add to that my inner critic arriving to berate me and it would only take things up a level (chaos included) and leave me feeling dejected, overwhelmed, worthless and full of shame. Sound familiar?

However, if I were able to meet myself moment to moment with compassion, everything would change. For example, if instead of calling myself an idiot and a child, and blaming myself for what had happened, I could soothe myself with kindness, understanding and empathy, the incident would have far less of an impact on me and my self-worth. Would the same be true for you?

Let's consider that for a moment. What would it be like to replace:

'You idiot, how could you be so clumsy? You're worse than a child. You're going to be late now and you've nobody to blame but yourself.'

With:

'It's okay, accidents happen. It's just coffee, it will wash out, don't worry. Let's see what we need in this moment to figure this out. Taking a deep breath and pausing to centre ourselves is probably a good place to start.'

Or (in reference to befriending your inner critic):

'I can see you're feeling stressed right now, and I get it, spilling coffee on myself was not part of the plan, but rather than berating me and criticising me, as this is something that could happen to anyone, I would love some kindness and guidance from you, please.'

Do you think one of the above tacks might change things for you, as much as I think it would change things for me?

REFLECTIVE PAUSE

Before we go any further, I invite you to pause here to check in with yourself about how the idea of self-compassion is landing with you. Does it sound interesting and helpful to you? Do you welcome it? Or is there a part of you that is resistant (for whatever reason)?

There is no right or wrong response here. Some of my clients welcome this work with open arms and a huge sigh of relief as suddenly they have a new way of being with themselves that feels warm and inviting. However, I am conscious that this kindness and understanding can be hard for some people to integrate into their lives, based on their comfort with the topic, their preconceptions of it, and the historical relationship they and their parents or caregivers had with compassion.

So: (a) Where do you fall on the spectrum? And (b) If the idea of introducing self-compassion into your life isn't exactly lighting you up, why do you think this might be?

To go back to Step Three Meeting your Inner Critic with Self-Compassion, the idea here is to meet your inner critic with self-compassion each and every time they appear so that this becomes a familiar process for you, just as criticising and judging yourself has been up to now. This process will support you and guide you rather than shaming you and leading you to feel negatively about yourself. And this process will be transformative in quietening your inner critic, this I promise you.

HEALING EXERCISE

Remember the exercise we completed in Stage One: Building Awareness of your Inner Critic, where you documented all your inner critic's judgements and digs? It's time to return to these notes and to respond to them.

For every single critical and judgemental comment you noted, I would love you to respond with a compassionate viewpoint. For example, if you wrote something like: 'You ate so much today, you glutton,' a compassionate viewpoint to take might be:

'I deserve to nourish my body and to treat it with kindness and respect. I am only human and some days I will have a bigger appetite or more cravings than others and that's okay, especially because I was tired today. I will look after myself by having a healthy and filling dinner tonight and by going to bed early.'

Take as long as you need to complete this exercise. You might finish it in a single sitting or you might return to it. The idea is to practise responding to your inner critic with compassion so that this process becomes more familiar and automatic for you. In time you will begin to organically respond with compassion every single time your inner critic appears. Good luck!

STEP FIVE SILENCE YOUR INNER CRITIC SUMMARY

At the beginning of Step Five Silence your Inner Critic I shared that inside all of us lies an inner voice that guides us. For most, this inner voice guides with judgement, shame and criticism, but it is entirely possible to transform this, so that instead our inner voice offers us guidance based on love, respect and deep compassion. Building a new relationship with my inner voice has been incredibly transformational for me, and by following the stages outlined above, this too is possible for you. So embrace these stages and live them. Build awareness to your inner critic, catch it each and every time it appears, and stop it, whether through mindfulness, affirmations, deep breathing or self-compassion. Commit to this work as deeply as you can and you will reap the rewards. This is the work and you absolutely have it within you to complete it. Remember, 'your inner critic is simply a part of you that needs more self love' (Amy Leigh Mercree).

STEP SIX

CULTIVATE COMPASSION

When we give ourselves compassion, we are opening our hearts in a way that can transform our lives
DR KRISTEN NEFF

Growing up, self-compassion was never a part of my life. No matter how hard I scan my memories, I can never recall meeting myself in this way. What I can recall is berating myself whenever I experienced a distressing emotion – 'You are far too sensitive, get over it' – words that led me to believe I was weak, flawed, and as if my internal world was something to invalidate and dismiss.

To be honest, I don't remember being met with compassion from other people either. That's not to say it wasn't there, but my memories are of people telling me how lucky I was, with the implication that I should be grateful for all I had been given in life. And I was incredibly lucky with the parents who adopted me, who adored me and devoted their lives to me. But looking back on my childhood and teens I now understand that while I was incredibly fortunate, I also experienced a significant trauma at the beginning of my life that deeply impacted me and has had a lasting emotional effect on me. Nowadays I can appreciate that I was placed for adoption out of love and a desire that I have a family with two parents who could provide for me, but as a child growing up with a deeply ingrained sense of unworthiness, I really struggled to feel that I belonged, that I was enough, and that my relationships were safe.

It was only in my early 30s that I was truly able to incorporate self-compassion in my life, a process that has been deeply healing for me and one that has changed my life (something I do not say lightly). You may recall from Step Five Silence your Inner Critic that the gift of self-compassion was given to me by a wonderful therapist named Bríd, to whom I will be eternally grateful.

One very pertinent example of this work was when I was describing to Bríd a grudge I held that I felt deeply ashamed of. I remember so clearly sharing that I didn't want to be the type of person to hold a grudge, and that I knew so innately the only person this was hurting was me, yet I couldn't seem to let it go, however hard I tried. Up to this point, as you can probably imagine, I was judging and criticising myself hugely for carrying this grudge, especially as I deemed the reason for it to be superficial and something I 'should' be able to just let go of. Yet my psyche was clinging tightly to it and holding me at war with it in the process.

During this admission Bríd asked me to dissect the grudge in minute detail, something I found deeply exposing. It felt so childish. I squirmed through the session and if I could have, I would have raced out the door never to return, but I stuck with it because I trusted Bríd and the process so fully and because I knew deep inside that this was the only way I could set myself free from the anger I was carrying. What astonished me was that when I told Bríd the story, her response was: 'Of course you feel angry about this.'

This simple sentence hit me like ton of bricks. How I was feeling was valid? It was okay for me to feel this way? I wasn't weak or at fault for carrying this emotional distress? With Bríd's help, very slowly I was able to build compassion for the anger I was carrying and to appreciate that my anger was a normal human experience, and one that we are all primed to feel. Suddenly, through offering myself this compassion, it felt like it was okay for me to feel this way. What's more, through asking myself what I needed in response to what had happened, I was able to understand the anger, work through it, and let it go. This was deeply healing for me, especially as whenever this grudge has since reared its head in my life, I have been able to meet it with compassion and understanding, something that softens it hugely for me time and time again.

UNDERSTANDING SELF-COMPASSION

If you want others to be happy, practise compassion.
If you want to be happy, practise compassion.
DALAI LAMA XIV

To understand *self*-compassion, we must first look at compassion. At its most basic the word 'compassion' means 'to suffer together'. I just love this concept.

REFLECTIVE PAUSE

Imagine meeting a friend and instantly seeing they are in distress. What do you imagine would happen for you in that moment?

Pause here to consider this for a moment.

I imagine during this reflective pause you thought you would very likely 'feel' it or 'for them', right? (Well, usually at least!) Not just that, but that you would (typically) also want to do anything within your power to alleviate their distress.

This is compassion. The desire to relieve suffering.

When considering compassion, empathy may also come to mind. However, while compassion is related to empathy, it goes one step further. When you experience empathy for another you tend to feel their pain and understand their perspective, whereas compassion includes the desire to help the person in their pain. Scientific research has found that when we experience compassion we release oxytocin, the 'love hormone', and areas of our brain linked to caregiving and empathy are activated and light up.

In Step Five we saw that self-compassion is the process of showering oneself with kindness, understanding and encouragement (and quietening the judgement and criticism that can be so automatic for us).

REFLECTIVE PAUSE

Does self-compassion feature in your life?

Spend a moment considering this before reading on.

REFLECTIVE EXERCISE

For all of us, offering compassion, kindness and understanding to a loved one is often far easier than offering it to ourselves. Let's consider this for a moment via an exercise inspired by one of self-compassion's leading researchers, Dr Kristin Neff:

1. Consider a time a close friend or family member opened up to you and shared that they were suffering. Using a pen and paper, write down how you responded to them in this moment. For example:

    - What did you do?
    - What did you say?

- What tone did you use when speaking to them?
- Can you remember how you felt towards them in this moment?

2. Now consider a time in your life when you were suffering. Note down how you responded to yourself in this moment and how you typically respond to yourself when experiencing struggle. For example:

- What do you tend to do when you are suffering?
- What do you typically say to yourself when you are suffering?
- What tone do you use to speak to yourself when you are feeling this way?
- How do you typically feel towards yourself when you are struggling in this way?

Spend a moment comparing these two scenarios. Do you notice a difference between the two approaches? If so, why do you think this is?

Consider also where you learned to offer your loved ones compassion and if this was something you were ever taught to offer yourself?

I encourage you now to reflect upon and note down how you think life might change for you if you were to begin treating yourself in the same way you treat your loved ones amidst their struggle.

What might it take for you to begin offering yourself the same compassion, kindness and understanding that you so freely offer to them?

We focused on our inner critic at length in Step Five Silence Your Inner Critic, and it is no accident that Step Six of our ten-step process is self-compassion-based. As I hope you've gleaned so far, self-compassion can play a huge role in softening and silencing our inner critic. Research also backs this sentiment, as it has found that when it comes to strengthening how we feel about ourselves, and our success and achievement in life, self-compassion is a far better alternative to criticising ourselves in the hope that it will motivate us to do better and try harder.

As I type, I'm mindful that when you are first introduced to the idea of self-compassion, it may feel self-indulgent or extremely foreign after years of berating and judging yourself. However, research has found it to be hugely transformative and one of the strongest markers of strength in the face of adversity and the ability to pick oneself up after a knock. Self-compassion has also been found to reduce self-judgement and self-criticism, as well as anxiety, depression and stress; increase mindfulness, optimism and overall well-being; act as a buffer against distressing experiences such as trauma; and to be one of the most powerful skills we possess for coping and resilience.

With all of these incredible benefits in mind, let's immerse ourselves in it.

HEALING EXERCISE

Practise this exercise in a safe space that is free from distractions. Get cosy, grab your favourite blanket and relax into the chair, floor or bed supporting your body. Settle in for a deeply healing journey.

To begin, gently close down your eyes and connect your awareness to your breath, taking slow and steady deep breaths in and out. Fall into a rhythm that feels natural to you and as you tune in to your breath and the rise and fall of your chest, notice how your body is responding to this nurturing stillness. All you have to do in this moment is breathe, everything else can wait. This is your time and if you notice your mind starting to drift off as we complete this exercise together, gently return your awareness to your breath and the rise and fall of your chest.

As you allow your body to fall into the natural rhythm of your breath, sink even further into the surface supporting you and connecting you to Mother Earth. This is your time. All the worries and thoughts that are circling in your mind can wait; it is time now to offer yourself love and compassion.

I invite you now, as best you can, to connect with something that has been weighing you down recently. Trust your inner wisdom in what comes to mind. Let it guide you. As it does, consider all the pieces of this exhausting puzzle. Notice them. Observe them. Pay attention to the shapes and space they fill. Feel your way into the situation that has been going on for you and how it has left you feeling. What thoughts arrive? Have any sensations appeared in your body? Take a moment to feel into this and into your ever-loyal body that breathes for you, carries you and supports you.

Whatever has arrived for you, this moment of struggle, of suffering, is difficult. This has been a lot for you to bear, a lot for you to carry. No wonder your shoulders have been feeling heavy and you have been feeling so tired. Of course you have been. In response to all you have been carrying, place your hands on your body to lovingly offer comfort. Feel their warmth. Their touch. Their soothing weight.

As you pause in this gentle moment, consider your humanness. The fact that all humans struggle. We all have down days and hard days, down weeks and hard weeks. As you pause here in this beautiful space you have created for yourself, spend a moment offering yourself some grace and compassion for all you have been carrying, for all you have been trying so bravely to bear.

How would you perceive a friend who has been carrying this burden? How would you meet them in their struggle, in their suffering? Can you spend a moment here offering yourself this love? This kindness? This gentle and accepting compassion?

Consider in this moment, in this stillness, in this space, what it is that you need to help you with the struggle and suffering you have experienced. What do you need to lighten the burden? To assist you as you journey on? What do you need? Spend a moment considering this and considering too how you can offer this to yourself. What gift can you bring with you from this stillness?

Once this is clear to you, again trusting whatever has arrived, as your inner wisdom is always here to guide you, I invite you to make a promise to yourself about how you can follow through with this gift. What do you need to implement it? How can you help yourself to achieve it? Spend a moment promising this to yourself. After all the burden and heaviness you have been experiencing, you so deserve to give yourself this gift, so here and now, in the presence of this safety, commit to it, for you, from you.

When you feel you are ready to return to the outer world, slowly start to shift your awareness back to the space you are in. Begin by gently wiggling your fingers and toes and then slowly stretch out your body, perhaps raising your arms above your head,

> bringing your shoulders to meet your ears, and then pulling your shoulder blades together behind you. Move your body in whatever way feels comfortable and inviting for you. When you feel ready, slowly open your eyes, coming back into the environment you are in. Check in with how you are feeling. Are you feeling relaxed, comforted and soothed? I really hope so, and if so, remember that you can return to this exercise anytime you need to.

This powerful and deeply healing exercise is one I use regularly with my clients, and one they go on to practise outside our sessions. I use it myself too when I am experiencing a struggle or a burden that feels heavy and unrelenting. I really hope this exercise is as powerful for you as it is for me, and that you choose to practise it as often as you need to. This is self-compassion, this is the work, and your healing journey will thank you deeply for offering yourself this kindness, understanding and love.

One of the main reasons I became a psychologist was to help others feel less alone on their journey, less alone than I once felt on mine. As a child, when people, or I myself, dismissed the struggle and suffering I was experiencing due to the hugely impactful trauma I underwent as a newborn baby, I felt weak, alone and flawed. However, since incorporating the gift of self-compassion into my life, I now meet the parts of myself that struggle from time to time with:

- Acknowledgement of how hard carrying this wound has been for me

- An understanding of how as a vulnerable human being who experiences a wide range of emotions (as we are all programmed to do) I of course struggle and suffer

- Kindness, love and acceptance for the experience I am going through

- And the all-important question: 'What do I need in this moment to alleviate my suffering?'

Often what I need in the moment (alongside self-compassion) is to sit with how I am feeling and to allow these emotions to circulate. Sometimes I need a hug and acknowledgement from a loved one that what I'm experiencing is hard but that I'm not alone in it. Sometimes a brisk walk is exactly what I need to release pent-up emotions; or I turn to somatic techniques, which I find incredibly soothing (perhaps now is a good time to journey back to Step Three to remind yourself of these). I also lean on a warm and nurturing mug of cacao and the journaling process to work through my emotions and release how I am feeling, or sometimes a good night's sleep is the cure.

REFLECTIVE EXERCISE

Write a list of five things that help you to feel better when you are feeling low or anxious, or experiencing emotions that are causing you distress.

Healing Tip: Often having a saved list like this is incredibly helpful as in moments of distress we can forget to turn to the things we know will help us. This can result in us engaging in behaviours that don't serve us or help us to feel any better and that we often regret engaging in afterwards.

SELF-COMPASSION BREAK

'You have peace', the old woman said, 'when you make it with yourself.'
MITCH ALBOM

When it comes to self-compassion and offering ourselves a moment of care when we need it most (rather than ignoring our needs and continuing with life, as we so often do), a really wonderful gift to offer ourselves is a self-compassion break.

As a parent, self-compassion breaks form part of my daily toolkit, as although my daughters are the most precious gift I've ever received, being a parent is the hardest thing I've ever done. I never knew before their arrival how something as small and as delicate as a newborn baby could test me so much, not to mention the sassy, spirited little characters they grow up to be. So I lean on self-compassion breaks daily, particularly when I feel I've failed them by losing my temper or not being the mum I try to be. A self-compassion break after a disastrous bedtime full of tears (mine and theirs) and tantrums, or a sleepless night, is exactly what I need to soothe and forgive myself, and the practice never fails me. The best thing about this healing exercise is that it can be completed in a very short time frame, yet can be incredibly powerful in helping you to pick yourself back up after a challenging moment or experience (or mini-me interaction!).

Although self-compassion breaks have only featured in my life since becoming a mother, I most definitely could have benefited from them long before, so whether you are a parent and can relate to the bedtime tantrums, or do not have children but still struggle to offer yourself the same kindness and compassion you offer to everyone else in your life, here is a step-by-step guide to enveloping yourself in a moment of self-care and love.

HEALING EXERCISE

Complete this exercise in a space where you feel comfortable and safe, and that is, if possible, distraction-free.

To begin, think of a situation or experience in your life that you are finding hard or that is causing you distress. Call this experience to mind as best you can, paying attention to any bodily sensations that arrive as you do so. To really benefit from this healing exercise, it is good to summon up some of the stress and discomfort that you have been experiencing due to this situation, so as best you can, while calling this to mind, welcome in the bodily sensations and feelings that arrive. Allow, too, the accompanying emotions. Perhaps fear, anger or sadness may come to you in this moment. Whatever emotions arrive are valid and welcome, there are no rights or wrongs here.

When you feel ready to do so, I invite you to say to yourself, whether silently or out loud, the following statements:

1. 'I am finding this really hard' / 'This is a moment of suffering' / 'I am really struggling with this' / 'This is really stressful / painful'. Choose the statement that feels most right to you, or come up with one of your own. The point of this step in the process is to home in on the mindfulness element of self-compassion so that we can recognise and lean in to the experience we are going through.

2. 'Suffering is a part of being human' / 'It's okay to feel this way, we all struggle from time to time' / 'I am not alone in my struggle, other people struggle too' / 'To struggle is to be human'

Again choose the statement that feels most comfortable and appropriate for you, or call to mind your own statement. This step's purpose is to help you remember your shared humanity and connection to others, in that none of us are perfect, we all struggle, make mistakes, and carry vulnerabilities and imperfections.

3. While placing your hand on your heart, 'May I be kind and compassionate to myself' / 'May I be patient and understanding with myself' / 'May I be gentle with myself' / 'May I be patient with myself and offer myself the compassion that I deserve'

Choose the statement that speaks to you most or create a new one for yourself. This step is designed to help you to be kind to yourself and to offer yourself the same patience, understanding and compassion you so easily and freely give to those around you.

4. 'What do I need in this moment to help me with this struggle?' / 'What can I do in this moment to help me with the burden I am experiencing?' / 'What can I do for myself to alleviate the suffering I am experiencing?' Or, very simply, 'What do I need in this moment?'

Select the statement that feels most comforting for you or find an alternative for yourself. In this step, consider what you need to assist you as you navigate this experience. Spend a moment reflecting on this and considering what gift you can bring with you from this exercise.

Complete this exercise whenever you need it, whether day or night. Ideally you'll have a private space to sit in while you do so but it is also available at other times, for example when sitting at your desk in work or when out in public. If you find yourself feeling emotional

> after completing this exercise, be gentle with yourself and take
> some time to soothe and care for yourself before returning to your
> day. And remember, take with you the gift you have promised
> yourself in the final step of your self-compassion break and
> honour this commitment to yourself as best you can.

Something I have found time and again since incorporating self-compassion into my life in a meaningful way is that it has helped me to reach a place of acceptance, both within myself and in relation to external factors in my life, that is often hard to reach without this helping hand. Self-compassion, and, indeed, compassion for others in my life (especially those who challenge or hurt me), softens me and helps me to widen my reference of understanding. I won't lie and say this happens instantaneously – often I have to sit with something and work through it before the softening comes – but I most definitely find it easier to arrive at this point of grace and acceptance when compassion is involved. This, for me, is 'the work'. The softening, the acceptance, the release of emotions that were previously flooding me. The ability to pick myself up and go on after a painful or wounding experience. I so hope that self-compassion can offer this to you too.

SELF-COMPASSION AFFIRMATIONS

I richly deserve to offer myself the same compassion and understanding I so freely give to others.

Another really powerful way to strengthen your self-compassion practice, and our final exercise of Step 6: Cultivate Compassion, is to introduce daily compassion-focused affirmations into your life. Positive or self-affirmations are statements or phrases that when repeated over time create new thought patterns and bring about intentional, positive change. This occurs due to the process of building new neural pathways and activating reward systems in our brain, something that leads us to seeking out the practice the more we do it. I have to admit that when I first discovered the practice of repeating positive affirmations to myself I was dubious, but after immersing myself in the science and incorporating the practice into my life I very quickly became a huge fan and reaped the rewards that came hand in hand with my new habit.

Have you ever immersed yourself in the practice? If you have, you will love this next healing exercise. If you are new to the concept, I am excited to introduce you to it and to share in your first experience. As I always say, nothing changes unless we make a change, so engage in the process as best you can with an open mind and an open heart, and enjoy.

HEALING EXERCISE

To begin, take a deep breath and recite your affirmations slowly and clearly out loud. Allow yourself to absorb the positive energy of the words you are speaking to yourself as best you can. Repeat each affirmation three times.

Carry out this exercise every day for 21 days, using five of the suggested affirmations below or choosing your own. To help you successfully incorporate this new habit into your life, I encourage you to spend a moment considering what time of day would be best for you to complete this task, and to stack it onto a habit you already have. For example, you could complete this exercise first thing in the morning as you get out of bed, while preparing your lunch or as you are brushing your teeth at night time.

'When things don't work out as planned, I offer myself compassion and understanding.'

'I am gentle and understanding with myself.'

'I offer myself the same grace I so easily give to others.'

'When things feel difficult, I remind myself that it's okay to struggle.'

'I am deserving of self-compassion.'

'My imperfections are what make me human.'

'I let go of all resentment I feel towards myself because of my past mistakes.'

'I am worthy of forgiveness and understanding.'

'I know that mistakes are part of being human.'

'I am patient and loving with myself as I learn and as I grow.'

STEP SIX CULTIVATE COMPASSION SUMMARY

When I consider the parts of my journey that have had the deepest healing impact on me, self-compassion is always the first one to come to mind. As you very likely gathered from this chapter, I feel very passionate about sharing the gift of self-compassion with others, as I believe so deeply in the practice and in the process. It is for this reason that I urge you from deep within my soul to offer yourself this beautiful gift, even if it feels extremely foreign to begin with; if you can find it within yourself to commit to the process as much as I have throughout my inner healing journey, I know without doubt that your life will change dramatically and unequivocally and I am so excited for you to experience this when the time comes.

So, be it via self-compassion breaks or positive affirmations, gently catching and challenging your inner critic with kindness, compassion and understanding, or by immersing yourself in the deeply healing meditation offered in this chapter, I hope self-compassion can soothe and comfort you and become as big a part of your life as it is of mine.

STEP SEVEN

STRENGTHEN YOUR SELF-WORTH

Over the years, I've interviewed thousands of people, most of them women, and I would say that the root of every dysfunction I've ever encountered, every problem, has been some sense of a lacking of self-value or of self-worth.
OPRAH WINFREY

For my entire life I felt 'shaky' in myself. It's a funny word to use, but it fits so completely. I felt shaky in my relationships. I felt shaky in my abilities. I felt shaky in what I had to offer the world or in how I could contribute. I felt shaky in my sense of self-worth. This shakiness followed me around like a dark cloud, and the worst thing about it was that I could so clearly see how special, talented and worthy everyone else around me was. It was almost like a special power; I'd spend five minutes with someone and I could see how brightly and vibrantly they shone. This never made me bitter, rather the opposite, in fact — I felt so lucky to sit in their sunshine — but I always felt that dark cloud above me in contrast to their light. In one way it was really beautiful, as I always saw those around me as their very best selves, their laugh, their lovable quirks, their uniqueness and the way they interacted with everyone and everything around them. But beside them, I felt like a dull shell of a person who never compared. This is the sad part of it, the really sad part, because as I type these words, I feel so sad for the little girl I carry inside, the little girl who never felt 'enough'. The little girl who always felt in the shadows. When I think of that little girl, that innocent, delicate little being, it fills me with so much sadness. Oh, how I wish I could have celebrated her right from the start, but that didn't come for many years. In fact it was only on becoming a mother myself, holding my precious newborn baby in my arms, seeing how special and perfect she was right from the start, that I could see I was too. My baby was so beautiful. So loved, and such a blessing to the world, as, I realised, I was too — I had just never realised it. There was nothing she needed to do, or to be, or to prove. She was born worthy and so fully and entirely 'enough'.

Just as I was, and just as you were.

Did you feel it? Did you view yourself in that way? Or did you feel shaky in yourself too?

In my early years as a psychologist I worked with a girl who was everything I wanted to be. Intelligent. Caring. Self-assured. When she spoke, people listened, and she always had something important to say. She was a gorgeous person inside and out and a wonderful psychologist. I never envied her, for I so enjoyed being in her company and I learned so much from her, but in comparison, I felt like a shadow beside her light. There was nothing that happened that led me to feel that way, we were never in competition or publicly compared, but it was my long-standing and deeply ingrained sense of never being enough (clever enough, pretty enough, self assured enough, worthy enough) that led me to feel I paled beside her in comparison.

I will never forget the first time I saw her after becoming a mother. As I hugged her I still saw her in all her splendour, for she really was the most gorgeous person inside and out, but in that moment, I had this life changing realisation …

So too was I.

She shone, but so did I. She was intelligent, caring, eloquent, beautiful, and a wonderful person and psychologist … but so too was I.

She shone and sparkled and contributed so much to the world, but so too did I.

It was never that there was only space for one of us to shine, and for one of us to sit in the shadows, and it was only in that moment that I really understood that there is space for us all to shine.

I realised that so fully in that moment, thanks to the gift my daughter gave me on her entrance into the world. That feeling intensified when I gave birth to my second child three years later — it was never that there was only space for one of them to shine, and for one of them to sit in the shadows; there was space for them both to shine in all their uniqueness and brightness and love.

What a gift that knowledge was, and it is a gift I hope I can pass on to you now as you read my words.

For you were born worthy. There was never anything for you to do, or say or to prove. You have always been enough, exactly as you are.

Now read that again, and soak it in this time.

You were born worthy. You have always been worthy. You will always be worthy.

You were born enough. You have always been enough. You will always be enough.

In fact, so much more than enough.

REFLECTIVE EXERCISE

As I share my story with you, I wonder how *your* relationship with *your* self-worth has been? Is it something you have always innately known and felt or have you too spent days, weeks, months, even years searching for it? Pause here to consider this and to complete this reflective exercise before reading on, perhaps reaching for a pen and paper to give this reflection the time and consideration it truly deserves.

Some questions that may help you to really reflect on your relationship with your self-worth are:

What words come to mind when you are asked to describe yourself?

Growing up, what value did you place upon yourself?

How do you feel about your value now?

Are your beliefs about yourself generally positive, negative or somewhere in between?

Where did your ideas and messages around your worth stem from?

After completing this reflective exercise, it is time to go on a healing journey.

HEALING EXERCISE

Practise this exercise in a safe space free from distraction. Get cosy, grab your favourite blanket and relax into the surface supporting your body. Settle in for a deeply healing experience.

To begin, gently close your eyes and connect your awareness to your breath, taking slow and steady deep breaths in and out. Fall into a rhythm that feels natural to you and as you tune in to your breath and the rise and fall of your chest, notice how your body is responding to this nurturing stillness. All you have to do in this moment is breathe, everything else can wait, this is your time. If you notice your mind starting to drift off as we complete this exercise together, gently return your awareness to your breath and the rise and fall of your chest, and if you would like an extra anchor in this moment, place one hand on your belly and the other on your heart and connect with the gentle movement of your body.

As you rest here, enjoying this moment of relaxation, I invite you to arrive even deeper in this moment with me. Sit in this moment in the entirety in your body. Feel the tip of your nose, your lips, feel each finger and the spaces between your fingers, feel your heart that beats just for you every single moment, feel your breath and the rise and fall of your body as it functions just for you, day in and day out. Feel all the life vibrantly alive inside you. Here in your beautiful body, here in your beautiful wholeness, it's time for you to remember your worth.

It's time to remember that you were born worthy. I know that worth is something you have been taught to search for, taught to prove, taught to demonstrate and to show. I know this is something that you've been taught to find ways to establish so that you are acknowledged and welcomed and heard, but this was an accident, a teaching impressed on you by those lost to their own worth, lost to their own beauty, lost to their own light. If you were to pause all your searching to uncover and gain all that you already are, how different would your life feel? Which parts of your wholeness and beauty would come alive and shine? If you were to innately know and believe that you are already perfect and in need of no changes, no trying, no effort, how would life feel different for you? How would you hold yourself? How would you be? How would you interact and engage and show up?

In all your trying you are simply revealing all that you have been all along. Your worth and your light and your brightness has always been here waiting for you to realise, to discover, to see. For you are so precious, and so loved and so whole, just by being you. It's time for you to remember now that all the ways you are trying to prove your worth are unnecessary, your search is unnecessary. In this moment, in the tip of your nose, your lips, your breath, your heart and the fullness of your very being, you are and always have been worthy. When was the last time you allowed yourself to just be? In all your authenticity and rawness? You have been worthy from the very moment you first took a breath cradled in your mother's arms. Breathe here, remembering your worth. Remembering your light. Remembering your beauty. Remembering the gift that is and has always been you.

So again I ask you, how different would your life feel, how different would your life be if you were to remember how innately precious and worthy you already are and have always been? How different would your life feel, how different would your life be if you never again felt the need to prove you are more than you already are, more than you innately are. For you are so perfect and precious and worthy just by being you. So lay it down. Lay down all the trying and proving and needing. Lay it all down, for you are so deeply tired of all of the searching and doing and effort. It is time for you to rest now. To rest in the remembering and in the knowledge that you were born so worthy and so precious and so enough. Rest in the remembering and in the knowledge of your value, your beauty, your immeasurable worth. Rest in the remembering and in the knowledge that you are loved, that you are deserving and that you have always been enough.

As you rest here now, safe and secure in your being, in your light, in the profound and undeniable worthiness you now know to be so true, you hear soft footsteps slowly approaching you. Footsteps that are so familiar to you. You turn your head softly and see the most lovely child before you. You drink in their perfectness. Their innocence, their pureness. You feel so much love for this little being, because this little being is you.

Drink them in as they stand before you now.

Their hair.

The expression on their little face.

Their little outfit and how they are holding themselves as they stand here with you.

As you breathe them in, they slowly come closer to you and suddenly you see the searching in their eyes.

The yearning.

The wanting.

The hoping.

For they want so much for you to remind them.

To remind them of all they have forgotten.

Of all they are already searching for.

So take a moment to lovingly do this for them.

To remind them how incredibly special they are.

To remind them how precious and worthy they are.

To comfort and care for and soothe them exactly as they are hoping you will.

They are getting sleepy now, this precious little being, and it is time for them to rest. Guide them by the hand to their bed. One where they feel safe and comforted and close to you.

Lovingly tuck them in and remind them that they are no longer alone, for you are with them now.

And just as they are drifting off to sleep, I want you to make a promise to this precious little soul.

A promise that you will no longer allow them to feel this way, to worry they are not enough. To worry they might fail. To worry that they will forever have to prove themselves.

Make this promise to them now as their eyelids begin to flutter.

Make this promise to yourself.

Allow yourself to rest here with them awhile, for you have nothing to do in this moment except be. Take as long as you need; this is your time.

When you feel rested and ready to return to the outer world, safe in the knowledge that you are and always have been so much more than enough, slowly start to shift your awareness back to the space you are in. Begin by gently wiggling your fingers and toes and then slowly stretch out your body, perhaps raising your arms above your head, bringing your shoulders to meet your ears, and then pulling your shoulder blades together behind you. Move your body in whatever way you need to and when you feel ready, slowly open your eyes, coming back into the environment you are in. Spend some time re-acclimatising to this space and to how you are feeling.

> This is deep, evocative work and can bring up many emotions and feelings, so be gentle with yourself and go about the rest of your day as slowly as you need to.

This powerful exercise is one I use regularly with my clients, and one they go on to practise outside our sessions. I use it too when feelings of 'not being good enough' creep up on me, as they sometimes continue to do, especially when I'm feeling vulnerable or threatened. Tapping into the knowledge and remembering that I *am* enough, and always have been, and grounding myself in this, really supports me to pick myself back up and begin again. I hope this beautiful healing exercise supports you to do the same.

SO WHAT DOES 'SELF-WORTH' ACTUALLY MEAN?

When we can let go of what other people think and own our story, we gain access to our worthiness – the feeling that we are enough just as we are and that we are worthy of love and belonging. When we spend a lifetime trying to distance ourselves from the parts of our lives that don't fit with who we think we're supposed to be, we stand outside of our story and hustle for our worthiness by constantly performing, perfecting, pleasing, and proving. Our sense of worthiness – that critically important piece that gives us access to love and belonging – lives inside of our story.

BRENÉ BROWN

Self-worth, self-esteem, self-confidence. We see and hear these terms all the time, but what do they actually mean? And, most importantly, what's the difference between them? As you may have already gathered, all three terms are related, but they reflect distinct and separate concepts. Let's begin with self-esteem and self-worth. Self-esteem is 'I do', whereas self-worth is 'I am'. For example, according to Dr Christina Hibbert, an expert in the area of self-worth, 'self-esteem is what we think and feel and believe about ourselves' (and our success and achievements in life based on judgements, thoughts, and feelings about ourselves), 'whereas self-worth is recognising "I am greater than all of those things." It is a deep knowing that I am of value, that I am lovable, necessary to this life, and of incomprehensible worth'.

Self-esteem is our appraisal of ourselves in comparison to others, while self-worth is an internal core belief of being of value and 'good enough' (good enough and worthy of love, good enough and worthy of all of the good things that happen in our lives, good enough and worthy to exist and take up space in the world), irrespective of external factors. So often we base our self-worth on external factors. Our success. Our career path. Our achievements. Our possessions. We strive and push and perform as best we can to prove that we are of value, but to what avail? And does all this effort actually achieve what we're hoping it will? When it comes to self-worth … no.

> *I know this story all too well because it sums up my life. I was the little girl who wanted to get ten out of ten in all of her spellings and maths tables. I was the teenager who wanted to score as many As as possible in school exams and distinctions in all of my music grades. I was the university student who strove to prove her worth by continuing her education until she reached the top, and by becoming the 'best' psychologist she could be. I was also the self-conscious young girl who compared her appearance and weight and clothes with her peers. The anxious girlfriend who watched on high alert to see if there were prettier and more interesting girls around the corner who might catch her boyfriend's eye. I always felt inferior so I continuously strove for better, bigger, more … and it was exhausting. Exhausting and relentless. For how could I ever stop to catch my breath when*

there was no real end in sight? I had set myself up on a never-ending hamster wheel and one I would never step off until I realised why I was continuously pushing myself so hard.

My story is proof that I was never going to build my self-worth via achieving and doing and climbing, and because my self-worth was so low, it was impossible to build any sense of self-esteem either, for I never compared. As I was never enough, or of worth, in my own eyes, how could I ever compare to others? How could I perceive myself to be doing a good job in any sense of the word if I didn't believe I deserved to take up space in the world or to be loved or valued or cared for by others?

As for self-confidence, the word 'confidence' derives from 'fidere', the Latin word for 'trust'; so in essence, our self-confidence reflects how much we trust our skills, knowledge and abilities. A good example of this is that I absolutely trust in my skills as a psychologist. I know I make a huge difference to my clients' lives and that I show up in my work in the way that I continuously strive to, as a kind, caring, nurturing and authentic supporter. However, this wasn't something I always felt. In fact, it is only since strengthening my self-worth, and in turn my self-esteem, that my self-confidence in my professional abilities (and in myself) has skyrocketed. Remarkably for me, I say this without fear of how it may be interpreted, when once I would never have dared to speak so highly of myself, because I believe so fully in my skills that even if someone were to read this and think 'Hmm, I'm not so sure', this wouldn't shake me, because after investing years of work in my inner healing, I know without doubt who I am and the value I contribute to my clients and, most importantly, to the world.

I share above that we will never build our self-worth through seeking it externally, as this validation and love needs to come from within for it to truly transform our relationship with ourselves and how we feel deep in our hearts. I would love to share an incredibly healing exercise with you that I first encountered many years ago as I embarked on my own self-worth journey. I was working with a therapist called Aileen at the time. Aileen was a character and very different from Maria, my previous therapist, from her dreadlocks and her crystals to the incense she burned and the Buddha statues she had around her therapy room. Sadly I didn't get to work with Aileen for long, as soon after we met my dad fell ill and I returned home to be by his bedside and soak him in for as long as I had left with him, but Aileen gave me one very beautiful gift that I will never forget, the gift I am going to now share with in the form of this deeply healing exercise.

HEALING EXERCISE

Let's begin.

I invite you to think of three very special people in your life. They can be anyone you trust and love and feel safe with, but really consider which three people you are going to choose, as your inner wisdom will tell you whether they are up for the very special job you are going to ask of them. Once you've decided, you are going to invite these three trusted people to write a very special list for you. A love list. A list of all of the things they deeply admire and adore about you. Keep it simple when you ask them to do this. If it feels safe to do so, you can explain that this request is part of your journey to deep inner healing, or perhaps you can think of another way to introduce your request that feels right for you. How you present it doesn't matter; all that is important is that you request this love letter and that when you receive it, you read it with an open heart, an open mind, warmth and gratitude. (Make sure to set the scene for yourself as you to do; this is going to be a hugely powerful experience and one you will never forget.)

I invite you to engage in this healing exercise because when I immersed myself in it at Aileen's request it was incredibly powerful for me. The words my boyfriend (now husband) and best friends wrote for me were so unexpected and so full of love that they took my breath away. I'll never forget reading them or the power they had, and although our self-validation must always come from within, what this exercise gifted me was hope. Hope that I could begin to see these things within myself. Something I have since gone on to do many times over; and I wish the same for you.

IT IS TIME NOW TO STRENGTHEN YOUR SELF-WORTH

Perhaps we just need little reminders from time to time that we are already dignified, deserving, worthy. Sometimes we don't feel that way because of the wounds and the scars we carry from the past or because of the uncertainty of the future. It is doubtful that we came to feel undeserving on our own. We were helped to feel unworthy. We were taught it in a thousand ways when we were little, and we learned our lessons well.

JON KABAT-ZINN

In my work as a psychologist, I sit with many people who deep down seek to feel worthy, to *be* worthy; but sadly, this is something that so few of us innately feel already. I share this because I imagine that you have also felt this way. It's really sad, isn't it? Where do we learn that we aren't enough simply by being ourselves? And why do we find ourselves searching so desperately to feel a sense of worthiness? Why isn't this something we simply possess, as we should? As we deserve. As our daughters and sons deserve too.

What has happened in our society that this is knocked out of us? Something that is so intrinsic for our success in life and, more important than anything else, for our happiness, is being denied to us. Why is that? Life grinds us down. It teaches us that we aren't enough. That we are lacking. That we need to do and be and prove more. As we journey through Step Seven Strengthen your Self-Worth together, what I wish from the bottom of my heart is that I can gift you the self-worth you so richly deserve. So whatever has happened to knock this out of you, if there is one thing you take away from Step Seven I hope it is this:

You *are* worthy.

You were *born* worthy.

There is nothing you need to *do* or say or *try* to prove your worth.

You are already enough and *so* worthy, just by being you. Your perfectly imperfect, messy self.

You *are* enough. This I promise you.

And actually, the only person you really need to convince of this is YOU.

And below I am going to share with you how you can start to do exactly that.

> **REFLECTIVE EXERCISE**
>
> Before we journey through *how* to strengthen our self-worth, it is important to pause and consider what or who it was that knocked it out of you. So reach for a piece of paper and a pen, and pause here to consider just this.

Was it someone from your early years?

A traumatic incident or event?

Or feeling continuously ridiculed time and time again?

Pause here to consider your 'why'.

Why has your self-worth been impacted?

What or who was a part of this?

Take your time here and give yourself the space you need to really consider this hugely important question ... and look after yourself in the process, for this work is hard. This work is deep. This work is where the healing truly stems from.

STRENGTHEN YOUR SELF-WORTH BY QUIETENING YOUR INNER CRITIC AND BUILDING SELF-COMPASSION

Choose, everyday, to forgive yourself.
You are human, flawed, and most of all worthy of love.
ALISON MALEE

When it comes to deep inner healing, strengthening your self-worth is truly transformative, because as Oprah Winfrey once very astutely said, 'at the root of every dysfunction I've ever encountered, every problem, has been some sense of a lacking of self-value or of self-worth'. I wholeheartedly agree with Oprah's inner wisdom, both because I have seen the incredible power this work offers through sitting with countless clients and watching their transformation, but also because of the deeply healing journey I have myself experienced since first recognising, on the birth of my newborn daughter, that I, like all of us, was born worthy with nothing to prove. The good news is that by allowing me to bring you on this ten-step healing journey you have already begun the process of strengthening your self-worth. By immersing yourself in the learnings of Step Five Silence Your Inner Critic and Step Six Cultivate Compassion, you have been working on this process and reaping the rewards it has to offer.

The reason for this is because to strengthen our self-worth we must first build awareness to the voice inside of us that judges us, criticises us, diminishes us and berates us. For how can we ever tap into and build our self-worth if we are telling ourselves that we are a failure, unworthy of anything and everything our heart desires? How can we feel good about ourselves and build our sense of value if we are belittling ourselves for our mistakes and struggles, despite us all, every single one of us, jointly experiencing them? So yes, quietening your inner critic and cultivating compassion are paramount for strengthening your self-worth and building your ability to truly and wholeheartedly believe you are enough, in fact so much more than enough.

Quietening your inner critic and cultivating compassion are so important in strengthening your self-worth that I suggest you pause here to revisit those two steps of our healing journey. Remind yourself of them and think how you can incorporate these powerful healing processes into your journey to strengthening your self-worth. Perhaps you could complete the suggested exercises for a second time or re-read the steps in their entirety. If you think it may benefit you to work on these steps further before incorporating them into Step Seven and then Step Eight, allow yourself the time to do this to truly embed the learnings these steps offer. Consider these processes a stepping stone along your pathway to deep inner peace and healing, stones you can journey back to before progressing further along your path. Remember, there is no rush; in fact, this work cannot and should not be rushed. It's a journey that promises huge results, so honour it and yourself and take the time you need to soak in as much of the magic as you can.

And remember: The effort you put into this process will be truly transformational.

Pause here to journey back to Steps Five and Six before continuing.

STRENGTHEN YOUR SELF-WORTH THROUGH SELF-AFFIRMATIONS AND NEUROPLASTICITY

Rewire your brain, rebuild your self-worth.

Neuroplasticity is the ability of our brain to form new neural pathways that shape and change our behaviours, beliefs and thoughts. The key to remembering your self-worth, the secret, the gold, is to repeatedly remind yourself of just how worthy you are. Over and over again. Even if you don't believe it. Even if it feels foreign. Even if it feels really hard. One very powerful way to do this is through affirmations, and one of my favourite affirmations, which I call upon often, is:

I am enough, I have enough, I do enough ... I have always been enough.

Repeat after me:

I am enough, I have enough, I do enough ... I have always been enough.

And again:

I am enough, I have enough, I do enough … I have always been enough.

Write it down too. Take it with you and remind yourself of it as often as you can, because it is absolutely true.

As we learned in Step Six Cultivate Compassion, self-affirmations are statements or phrases that when repeated over time create new thought patterns and bring about intentional, positive change. This occurs because when we build new neural pathways we activate our brain's reward system, which leads us to seek out the practice the more we do it. I love using affirmations to help me remember my worth, and the longer I have been using them, the more and more my belief in them has grown. This is a process I really trust, and one that the science backs, so try the healing exercise below with an open heart and an open mind and feel this wonderful healing power for yourself.

To help you to incorporate self-worth affirmations into your life, here are some more of my favourites:

- I am worthy of love and respect.

- I am deserving of all the good things life has to offer.

- I am comfortable being my true authentic self with others.

- I am proud of my accomplishments, big and small, and all I have learned along the way.

- I release the need for validation from others.

- I am worthy of forgiveness, including forgiveness from myself.

- I am worthy of giving and receiving love freely.

- I am worthy of respect, consideration, love and kindness from others.

- I am a beautiful person, inside and out.

- I deserve to take up space and express myself.

- I trust my intuition and make choices that align with my true self.

- I am valuable and irreplaceable.

HEALING EXERCISE

To begin, take a deep breath and, slowly and clearly, recite aloud your affirmations (or a number of the affirmations above). Allow yourself to really absorb the positive energy of the words. Repeat each affirmation three times.

Carry out this exercise every day for twenty-one days, using five of the suggested affirmations above or choosing your own. To help you successfully incorporate this new habit into your life, I encourage you to spend a moment considering what time of day would be best for you to complete this task, and to stack it onto something you already do. For example, you could complete this exercise first thing in the morning as you get out of bed, while preparing your lunch or as you get into bed at night.

Once you have become comfortable with this healing exercise, I recommend you deepen it even further by beginning to recite your affirmations in front of the mirror. Stand tall as you do so, and speak each affirmation with intention and power, soaking in the energy that flows as you recite these healing words. If this feels exposing or difficult at first, fake it until you make it, because you will make it, and soon you will be speaking these words confidently and with absolute certainty.

Good luck over the coming 21 days. I am so excited for you to experience the power that affirmations bring, especially in strengthening your self-worth.

STRENGTHENING YOUR SELF-WORTH THROUGH SELF-LOVE PRACTICES

You yourself, as much as anybody in the entire universe, deserve your love and affection.
BUDDHA

SELF-LOVE DIARY

Another extremely effective technique to strengthen your self-worth is to keep a self-love diary and to write down three things you love about yourself (or three things about yourself that you are grateful for) every single day. Things like how loving you are. How determined you are. How resilient you are. How funny you are. How good at hugs you are! This technique will likely feel very foreign to you as you incorporate it into your life – we rarely consider and celebrate ourselves in this way – but it is an incredibly powerful technique. In fact, it is far more powerful than you may believe it to be until you experience it for yourself. So trust me on this technique, and complete it because I am asking you to. I promise you that you WILL notice a change if you engage in it.

To help you remember to complete this healing exercise on a daily basis, leave your diary on your bedside locker and make it a non-negotiable practice. My clients love this technique because the change it brings is so huge if you can commit to it. So commit to it. Take this as a gift, and one that WILL change things for you.

REFLECTIVE PAUSE

Three things I love about myself are:

1.

2.

3.

Three things about myself that I am thankful for are:

1.

2.

3.

Complete this reflective pause before reading on.

SELF-LOVE NOTES

Another brilliant technique to strengthen and remind yourself of your self-worth is to grab a mirror marker or some Post-it notes and write down reminders for yourself in places you will see them often. Think your bathroom mirror, your bedside locker, on the front of your laptop or notebook, or on the sun visor of your car. Similarly, you could save something meaningful as a phone or laptop screensaver. Repeated exposure to your notes will remind you of how worthy, how unique and how good enough you are (and have always been).

Remember, these exercises are all about repetition and building those new self-worth neural pathways. So celebrate yourself. Big yourself up. Remind yourself of how special, how worthy, and how more than enough you are and always have been.

SELF-LOVE LETTER

One final self-love exercise that I highly recommend you engage in as you continue along your journey of embracing and celebrating yourself in all your glory (and in turn, changing your life) is to write a heartfelt love letter to yourself. Do this at a time when you feel calm and full of love, perhaps after a warm mug of cacao (my favourite heart-opening plant medicine), and follow the instructions below as I guide you to offer unconditional love and affection to the most important person in your life – you.

HEALING EXERCISE

First set the scene for this exercise. For example, write outside as you sit in nature, breathing in the scents and sounds of your surroundings, or inside in a cosy haven where you can dim the lights, burn your incense and candles and get cosy with a warm blanket and your favourite pyjamas.

Reach for your journal or a fresh sheet of paper, and your favourite pen, and settle in for a deeply healing experience. If you are nervous or unsure of where to begin, trust your heart, your soul and all the love you have to offer yourself, even if you don't fully believe that this love will flow for you as freely as it does for everyone else in your life. Trust the process, trust your inner wisdom and allow whatever happens to happen. This is the process. This is the journey. This is the healing.

Part 1: Write a love letter to a much younger version of yourself. As you put pen to paper, really bring to life this little you. Their hair. The outfit they are wearing. Their little hands and their little feet. The expression on their face. How at ease they are – or the complete opposite! Soak them in as they arrive into your mind and into your heart, and then put pen to paper and write. Write them a letter telling them everything you love and admire about them. Pour your heart out as fully and as wholly as you can. Write all the things you wish you could have felt and believed and heard when you were this precious little being. Write all the things you know they want to hear. Write and send as much love their way as you can.

Part 2: When you feel ready, read the love-filled letter you have written to this much younger version of yourself you carry inside you. Soak in the words with every sentence you read. Allow the love and affection to envelop you and welcome in the energy that flows. If tears flow too, allow them, for they are so healing, and often so needed. Go gently and slowly and take as much time as you need. This is deep and powerful work and you are so brave to engage in it.

Part 3: When you have completed Parts 1 and 2, I invite you to complete the final piece of this deeply meaningful healing exercise. Do so at a time that feels right. If immediately after completing Parts 1 and 2 doesn't feel like the right time, allow yourself to listen to your inner wisdom and to come back to this final step when you feel ready and open to doing so. When that time arrives, I invite you again to read this love-filled letter, but this time I want you to imagine, as best you can, that you are reading these words to your current self, the adult you are right at this moment. Read these words and allow them to envelop you. Read them with as much belief as you can muster, and as you do, allow the words and the love and affection to soak into your heart. What a powerful gift to give yourself.

Be gentle and loving with yourself as you go on this journey, and keep this letter safe so you can return to it when you next need a reminder of your beauty and light, or feel free to write this letter again, time and time again in fact, for each version of it will be just as powerful and just as healing as the first time.

STEP SEVEN STRENGTHEN YOUR SELF-WORTH SUMMARY

When I'm feeling vulnerable and my inner critic questions or admonishes my self-worth (it's like she awaits any sign of vulnerability and pounces as soon as one arrives!), I am so practised now at counteracting my inner critic and everything she has to say, because of how familiar I am with the techniques outlined above. For this reason I catch my inner critic and her criticisms almost as quickly as they arrive; and in doing so I remind myself that actually *I am enough*. *I am worthy* and *I am deserving* of all of the good in my life.

Just as you are.

Because of all of the healing work I have done over time, and with lots of practice, I have grown to believe this more and more, so these thoughts have become even more automatic and powerful for me. So, dear reader, if you try these deeply healing techniques and strategies I am prescribing for you now, and commit yourself to them as wholly as you can, you too will come to believe and feel their power. This I promise you.

Because:

- This work *will* change your life.

- This work *will* bring deep inner healing.

- And, most importantly, this work *is* the work.

So give it a try … you can thank me later.

As we bid farewell to Step Seven Strengthen Your Self-Worth, I leave you with one of my favourite poems that sums up so beautifully everything I have shared with you above. Read it and read it again. Mark this page as one to come back to, and when you need reminding of just how worthy and 'enough' you truly are, soak in these words:

YOUR LIGHT
DONNA ASHWORTH

Your light does not come from your successes.
Your light is not ignited by perfection,
or achievement
or body shape.

Your light is not fuelled by popularity or acceptance.
Neither is your light at any risk of being put out,
when other lights around you are bright.

Your light is simply made of the you-ness that makes you you,
the worries you have in the night,
the music which sparks your joy,
the books you had to read twice,
the memories stored safely in your heart,
the people you love and the people who love you.

Your light is never dependent on how you look
or how you perform.
it's just there
and it's quite simply brilliant
and it's all yours.

And it lights up every room you walk into
whether you activate it or not.

What a wonderful thing.

Shine bright little fighter
this dark world needs your glow.

STEP EIGHT

CULTIVATE CONNECTION

*Connection is why we're here.
It is what gives purpose and
meaning to our lives.*
BRENÉ BROWN

For as long as I can remember I've craved connection. Growing up, I yearned for it constantly. I would see other people so at ease in their relationships (and in themselves) and wonder, how can I achieve that? It never came easy for me. I was always on high alert. Always on edge. Always watching from the sidelines and never simply present and immersed. Looking on from the outside, I don't think you would have known this about me. I was surrounded by parents who adored me, a big and boisterous extended family, and plenty of friends, but I never felt I truly belonged or that it was safe to give myself up to them, because I had experienced the pain of rejection and abandonment once before and so there was always a part of me hypervigilant to the fact that this might happen again.

I was also disconnected from myself. I lived heavily in my head, with anxiety and rumination ever present. I yearned so much for connection that instead of assessing how I felt about the situations and experiences I was navigating, I was constantly switched on to the other and how I thought they would want me to be. I assessed that my parents would want me to be a good little girl; that my teachers would want me to be committed and to achieve good results; that my friends would want me to be fun and humorous and interesting; that boys would want me to be pretty and submissive and focused only on them. What did I aspire to? What did I want to be and to do and to say? Who knows. I certainly didn't, in fact I never gave it a moment's thought, so preoccupied was I by others and their desires.

I really struggled with intimacy. Not in the romantic, physical sense, but in being seen, in being heard, in being vulnerable with another, in lowering my mask and in sharing my soul. I was so guarded and on such high alert that I always held back, watching on from the sidelines and assessing how I should be and the dynamics that were at play. I'll never forget going on my first holistic wellness retreat. I felt so incredibly exposed. The moment I arrived I knew the retreat facilitators could 'see' me, deep into my soul, and that terrified me. What would they see? Would I be who and what they expected of me? Who and what I needed to be to fit in and to be 'enough'? My week on that Italian retreat changed my life because it allowed me day by day to slowly and cautiously open myself up to being seen in a way I had never risked before. Surrounded by the most beautiful and loving women, on that retreat I bared myself in all my entirety in a way I had never done before, and in that, the most incredible thing happened, because in the eyes of the women I was surrounded by I saw myself reflected back in a way I never had before. I saw my light. My pureness. My beauty, inside and out. My worth. I went home from that retreat a changed woman, and I have carried with me since the gift that each and every single woman I shared that unforgettable week with gave me.

THE IMPORTANCE OF CONNECTION

We cannot live for ourselves alone. Our lives are connected by a thousand invisible threads, and along these sympathetic fibres, our actions run as causes and return to us as results.
HERMAN MELVILLE

One of my favourite longitudinal research projects, the Harvard Study of Adult Development, sheds a huge amount of light on the importance of connection in our lives. Ongoing since 1938 (making it the longest scientific study of adult life ever conducted!), this research project has been investigating what makes people flourish in their lives (in other words, what makes people grow and evolve and live a meaningful and fulfilling life). The study's initial sample was 725 men from Boston. As time passed, these men's families were invited into the study so that it encompassed their partners and children too. Since 1938, participants' emotional, mental and physical health have been monitored via questionnaires and interviews; blood testing, body scans and DNA studies; as well as photographs, audiotapes and videotapes. The results of this study are fascinating, and I would highly recommend you take a look if it's of interest to you. The main finding from this study that has been ongoing for 87 years is that the people who lived the healthiest and longest lives, and were the happiest and most fulfilled, were those who maintained the strongest connections with others, be it romantic partners, their children, relationships with their family of origin, like their siblings and parents, work colleagues, or friends they felt strong and meaningful bonds with. In addition, the people who identified as having positive relationships in their lives were less likely to develop physical health difficulties and also experienced a later and slower onset of cognitive decline; and those who married lived, on average, five to twelve years longer if female, and seven to seventeen years longer if male. Isn't that incredible?

Something that also really interested me, was that when the first tier of participants entered their eighties they were asked what regrets they had about how they had lived their lives, and also what they were most proud of. The male participants most commonly responded that they regretted spending so much time in work and not enough with their families, while the female participants regretted the amount of energy they gave to wondering what other people thought of them (sounds familiar!). For all participants, their proudest achievements all related to their relationships and the most important people in their lives. Isn't that beautiful?

THAT WHICH INTERRUPTS CONNECTION

Trauma compromises our ability to engage with others by replacing patterns of connection with patterns of protection.
STEPHEN PORGES

Connection, by definition, is a feeling of closeness and belonging, both to oneself and to those around us. As an adopted person, like many people who experienced a significant separation or trauma in early childhood, I really struggled with a sense of belonging growing up, so it makes a lot of sense that connection and closeness were things I yearned for all my life. This sense of disconnection, and the struggle to perceive closeness and to feel like I belonged will, I imagine, be understood by many people as it is something I see in my therapy room almost daily. Not everyone who experiences these struggles has an early attachment wound like the one I have carried since my entry into the world, but I am of the firm belief that people who develop this struggle do so for a reason. The reason may be related to a hugely significant trauma, like the loss of a parent or the experience of living with a parent who has an addiction difficulty, or an experience of childhood abuse, or it may be a smaller but prolonged 'little t' trauma such as emotional neglect, verbal abuse, bullying or continuously feeling dismissed, unheard and unimportant. A sense of disconnection may also present due to psychological and cognitive difficulties, medication use, substance abuse or a deficit in social skills.

Note: A 'little t' trauma can be a very impactful and distressing experience but one that does not fall within the scope of a 'Big T' trauma. Examples of 'Big T' traumas include natural disasters, witnessing a violent crime or serious accident, or experiencing a severe illness.

REFLECTIVE EXERCISE

In a space that feels safe, reach for a pen and paper and consider how connected, or indeed, disconnected you have felt across your lifetime.

Are there certain periods that stand out for you when you consider this question?

Are there certain people who come to mind, perhaps some you have felt connected to and others you have not?

Has anything happened in your life that has impacted your sense of connection and belonging?

Where do you stand now in relation to feeling connected to those around you, and to yourself?

Does anything get in the way of your sense of connection now? If so, what?

Pause here to consider these questions and to put pen to paper as you explore them in as much detail as you can. Be gentle with yourself throughout this exercise and in the aftermath. Reflecting on topics such as this can be painful and evocative, so take it as a pace that feels right for you and look after yourself throughout the process.

Something else that can cause us to feel hugely disconnected in life is our lifestyle and how present (or unpresent) we are in the moment, from day to day and from month to month.

When I think back on how I have lived my life, I can now see how preoccupied I always was and how full my mind has always been. In secondary school I felt such pressure to achieve and to fit in that during my final school exams I was so wound up and feeling so anxious that I wouldn't achieve the grades I needed that I was a living nightmare for my parents. I had been the little girl who never gave a moment's trouble (I was the daughter who used to tell them when we were 'sneaking out' or 'going drinking'!), but during my exams I was cheeky, demanding and completely consumed by the pressure, with no awareness that the world didn't just revolve around me.

Fast forward to my degree, master's and doctorate and I again found life to be extremely overwhelming and oh so busy. Planning my wedding felt the same, full of pressure and deadlines and stress. This hugely took away from the beauty, joy and excitement of the time, even up to the day before the wedding, when I was ordering my bridesmaids around and tying 180 bows on napkins!

Fast forward again to my first year of motherhood, both with my first and my second baby, where my mind was consumed by the long nights, developmental leaps and needs of my beautiful newborns. I found the year following the birth of my second daughter particularly challenging as she was a reflux baby who slept for 40-minute internals at night, was too poorly to nap during the day, and constantly regurgitated her feeds. She lost so much weight in the first few months of her life that she had to undergo tests to rule out serious illness. I will never forget holding her down in a hospital room as they drew blood from my tiny helpless little baby. How I survived that period I will never know. I most definitely experienced postpartum anxiety as a result, something you would think a psychologist would have picked up on, but because I was so 'in it' I really didn't.

I share my story with you to highlight how disconnected and unpresent we can feel due to our life circumstances, but also (and mainly) due to the chaos of our minds.

For example, life for me has always felt like a never-ending treadmill of 'I just need to get to next week until things will feel easier', but of course 'next week' never came, as there was always something else. Things really hit rock bottom for me towards the end of 2023. I ended the year feeling incredibly burnt out and disconnected from everything and everyone in my life, including myself. I felt so down and so low, guilty because I wasn't available for anyone in my life in the way that I wanted to be, especially when it came to Paul and my gorgeous girls, and paralysed with exhaustion. I talked to one of my most trusted friends about it at the time and realised in that moment how hard I was pushing myself ... but to what avail? What was I aiming for? Why was I caught in this cycle? Was I living my life aligned to my values and the things that were important to me? Absolutely not. I yearned for a life that felt peaceful, joyful and connected, yet I was feeling anything but. I spent the final month of that year sitting with a cup of cacao and my trusty journal, and meditating and reflecting on how I could make a change to my life and calm the chaos of my mind. This would be my gift to myself and to my family, and when it came to my health, both physical and mental, it was incredibly needed. However, I won't lie to you, even with all the new awareness that was seeping in, I felt very stuck in how to actually make a change, because for so long I had lived in this way. For so long, my ambition and drive and low self-worth were pushing me to achieve and to 'do' and to succeed. So if you too have ever felt stuck on that never ending treadmill, I know how incredibly hard it is to make a change that will actually last.

In the end, it was the Universe and a very special soul who transformed things for me. That December I fell pregnant with my third baby, and come January, February and March I was completely bedbound with hyperemesis gravidarum and had no choice but to slow to a standstill. During my waking hours I thought of nothing else but the fear that flooded my mind. How would I survive financially when I was self-employed and bedbound? Would everything I had worked so hard for be threatened as I had to say

'No' to every opportunity that arose? I had wanted to feel more connected to those in my life, yet I was now in bed 24/7, too ill to even pick up my phone, never mind stay in touch with people or be present for my little girls in the way that they needed me. This period was extremely difficult. I had been so excited to see that 'plus' on the pregnancy test and to tell Paul this incredible news on a beach in Mexico as the sun rose, yet a month or two later it felt as though my life was falling apart. I felt so blessed to be pregnant, especially as I grew up in a home where this was not possible for my parents, but also so incredibly hopeless, and I will never forget sitting in the maternity hospital begging for support as the tears clouded my eyes and my body rocked in sickness and despair. If you have experienced hyperemesis gravidarum you will understand how debilitating and lonely an experience it is, and those three months were some of the toughest of my life.

What this period taught me, however, was that the world kept spinning, despite me having to surrender to stillness in every way imaginable. Life went on. My girls continued to thrive. My relationships survived, even though I was unable to nurture them. My business navigated the storm. Shortly after my sickness began to subside, I was very lucky to go on a beautiful holistic wellness retreat. While there, and in the months since, I repeatedly received the same message: To Surrender. To Trust. To Let Go. This pregnancy was sent to me to bring me to a standstill so I could reset and see the bigger picture. Ever since, I have been living a much slower-paced life (which my nervous system has been loving) because this period of stillness taught me to connect inwards more deeply, and to listen to the whispers within. You see, our body, heart and soul are always guiding us if we can just slow down enough to pay attention to their messages. This period of stillness also taught me how to say 'No' without guilt and without fear. It also taught me the value of slowing down, and it showed me what living with a regulated nervous system felt like. This life lesson introduced me to calm and peace I have never felt before, and it changed my life.

In sharing my story with you I hope I can inspire you to consider how you can give yourself permission to slow down, and in doing so, become more connected to yourself and to those around you than you have ever been before. This is my wish for you, and one I will hold in my heart as you read my words and consider your lifestyle, and chaos of the mind, and how, baby step by baby step, you can begin to live a slower-paced and more connected and fulfilling life. As part of this, I share below some words that recently came to me while sitting with my journal and a mug of cacao. Words that remind me of how deeply healing it is to tune inwards and connect with my body, heart and soul; a sentiment I always share with my clients and the attendees of my healing events to help them too to connect inwards and to begin to untangle the chaos of their minds. I hope reading these words are as powerful for you as they are for me.

TAKE A BREATH

Close your eyes
Take a breath
And feel the peace arrive
With each inhale
Your shoulders melt
And your soul becomes alive

Within this pause
Within this space
Where all your flurries still
You'll find a sense of knowing
And of the power
You hold within

For here is home
And here is love

With your hand placed on your chest
So connect within
Place your worries down
And allow yourself to rest

As this is where
The healing comes
And the untangling
Of your heart
So allow yourself this time, my love
Before making a fresh start

DISCONNECTION AND LOW MOOD

Depression is the ultimate state of disconnection, not just between people but between one's mind and one's feelings.
PARKER J. PALMER

Low mood or depression is characterised by feelings of disconnection, isolation and loneliness. Symptoms include feeling sad and teary, hopeless and helpless, worthless and worried, irritable, guilt-ridden, and lacking energy and motivation for all the things that previously made up your daily routine and that you found enjoyable in life. There can be many contributing factors to experiencing low mood. Things like age, genetics, traumatic experiences, medications, conflict, the death or loss or someone or something important to you, having to suppress yourself in some way, a major life change, or substance abuse. Low mood lies on a spectrum, from the typical bouts of feeling down that can hit all of us from time to time (for example when we're tired), to mild, moderate or severe clinical depression. Often people will ask me, 'How do I know if this (anxiety, depression, trauma, high cortisol levels) is a problem for me or that it's time to seek help?' and my answer is always the same: 'if something is interfering with your life or happiness levels, you owe it to yourself to do whatever you can to feel better.' Support is so readily available, and despite how you are feeling about yourself now, you deserve, and are worthy of, support and love and care. Depression has entered my therapy room many times and every single time I have noticed one huge similarity in all the people who have sat before me – disconnection. Disconnection from themselves, from those around them and from the world. Let me share a story with you that really highlights this.

I once worked with a man called Thomas who was in prison, having committed a very serious crime. On our first meeting, Thomas walked into the room with his eyes averted to the floor. He sat down opposite me and after a very brief glance in my direction, his eyes again trailed to the blue carpet beneath our chairs. Thomas was very polite and mannerly as we engaged that day, and presented so differently from the man who came across in the many newspaper articles I had seen when he was arrested. Over the course of a year Thomas and I worked together week-on-week and it quickly became apparent to me how disconnected and alone he had felt all his life, despite constantly being surrounded by people and growing up in a large, chaotic family.

Because of his disconnection and isolation in life Thomas never really learned how to appropriately engage with others, whether one-on-one or socially. As he struggled academically in school, he was never met with kindness there either, something which exacerbated things for him and led to him leaving school at a very early age. As a teenager and young man, Thomas always felt anxious in his interactions with others and never quite knew how to act or what to say. This caused great difficulty in his life and in his quest for connection, and from an early age he turned to drink and drugs to ease his discomfort and numb his loneliness. Thomas eventually ended up homeless, living on the streets and spending the little money he came across on cheap beer and vodka. His disconnection and isolation intensified while he was living rough and he would often intentionally commit petty crimes to bag a warm bed and a hot meal in prison. During our work together, as well as focusing on strategies to reduce his violent behaviour and lower his risk of reoffending, we also worked on integrating him back into a sense of community (community being the workshops and social outlets available for him in prison – Thomas was serving a very lengthy sentence) and on his sense of disconnection and loneliness. We started slowly and practised his social skills and comfort in engaging with others. We also worked on his self-worth, his low mood, his emotional awareness and intelligence and his anti-social beliefs and behaviours.

Over time, Thomas flourished. He no longer continually gazed at the floor while we talked and slowly made friends on his prison landing and in the prison school. He set goals for himself, both those he could achieve while in prison, but also those he could aspire to on his eventual release. His low mood improved considerably, and he began to feel so much more connected to himself and to those around him. His body posture changed, as did his appearance; he started taking better care of himself and his personal hygiene, and he no longer presented as the downcast, hopeless man I had set eyes on the day we first met. When I was transferred to another prison our work together ended, but during our final session Thomas thanked me profusely for being so kind and supportive and for the huge growth I had helped him achieve. Through our therapeutic relationship and his finally feeling that someone cared about him, Thomas had found his self-worth and had begun to engage in life in a way he had never done before. In doing so he found connection, companionship, happiness and, most importantly, himself.

STRATEGIES TO LOWER DEPRESSION AND DEEPEN CONNECTION

Only through our connectedness to others can we really know and enhance the self. And only through working on the self can we begin to enhance our connectedness to others.
HARRIET LERNER

Anyone who has experienced depression will know how incredibly debilitating it is. The hopelessness, the helplessness, the worthlessness, the despair, the insomnia, the constant bone-aching tiredness, the feeling *so* low and so despondent. And the worst part? Feeling like you will forever be in this dark hole. It's excruciating, it's soul-destroying, and it's a very, very lonely place to be. I think what makes it worse is that the ways out of depression feel so out of reach when you're in that dark hole. Exercise? 'How do you expect me to exercise when I can't get out of bed?' Connect with loved ones? 'How do I do that when I can't even shower and the thought of seeing someone and sharing how I've been feeling fills me with absolute dread?' Mindfulness? 'You've got to be kidding me, I don't want to be alone with my thoughts right now. I feel so worthless and so hopeless and in the darkest bubble of my life, there's no way I'm practising mindfulness.'

So what can you do? That's a good question, a really good question. The answer I always give is to start with your doctor. Go for a chat. Tell them how you feel, talk it over with them, including your treatment options (and treatment options doesn't always mean medication, by the way, it can mean therapy, exercise, meditation, yoga, integrating socially). See it as your first step, and go from there. Things *will* start to feel easier with this first step, I promise you, so take the first step, because so often people wait. 'I might feel better in a week or two, I'll suffer on for another little while, things will start to feel easier soon'. But actually they probably won't, not unless you take a step towards feeling better, towards seeing the light at the end of the tunnel.

Awareness of why you are feeling the way you are feeling is also incredibly helpful, so I'll share with you a very powerful exercise you can complete to support you with this. It's one I regularly use with my clients that is really impactful for them, and I hope it offers you as much support as it does them.

HEALING EXERCISE

Part One
The first step of this healing exercise is to reflect on four (or more, if they arrive for you) key life experiences that have shaped you and characterised your journey to today. To give you an example from my life, being given up for adoption is without doubt one of the defining moments of my life, as is the death of my father.

What are four key life experiences that have shaped your life and your journey?

Pause here to complete this step before moving on to part two.

Part Two
Reflect on four (or more, if more than four arrive for you) experiences or key factors that have shaped your low mood or depression story. What might help with this is to consider where your experience with low mood or depression started, or perhaps what triggered it. Consider too how your low mood or depression story has evolved and some realisations you've had along the way. Add as much richness as you can here. The more pieces of the puzzle you can pull together the better.

Pause here to consider all of the above. Take as long as you need, there is no rush.

Part Three

Now track all of the experiences you have noted along your life timeline (the four or more factors you flagged as part of your key life experiences, and the four or more factors you flagged as part of your depression story). To do this, plot out a timeline from when you were born up to now, marking along the way these eight or more significant points of your life. This will likely be a very impactful and eye-opening exercise for you, so take your time and be gentle with yourself. This work is hard but so incredibly worthwhile.

Pause here to complete this step before moving on to the final part of this healing exercise.

Part Four

The final part of our healing exercise is to plot on your life timeline four changes you would like to manifest in your life, or four goals that feel really important to you. Spend time really considering these hopes and aspirations. Make sure they feel meaningful to you and that they are not impacted by external pressures.

Once you've completed this step, I invite you to select one of your goals or desires and to make a step-by-step plan of how you can start to bring this goal or dream to life. This aspiration might be to start to feel better in yourself; to take the first step by making an appointment with your GP; or it may be something completely different and hugely ambitious. There is no right or wrong here, just something that feels important and meaningful to you, so let your inner wisdom guide you with this. The sky is the limit.

Once you have completed this exercise I encourage you to keep your work to look back on. You will have gathered such rich information. If it feels right to you, you could bring these pages to your doctor or therapist to talk through, or to your partner or a loved one to help them really understand how you are feeling and what has shaped you into the person you are today. I really hope this exercise brings you clarity, comfort and healing. Taking time to complete exercises such as these is deeply beneficial and although you may not necessarily jump at the chance of doing them, investing in this work will pay huge dividends for you.

ENGAGING IN THERAPY TO CULTIVATE CONNECTION

I define connection as the energy that exists between people when they feel seen, heard, and valued; when they can give and receive without judgement; and when they derive sustenance and strength from the relationship.
BRENÉ BROWN

Brené Brown's words describe my beliefs about therapy so beautifully and wholly because, as a psychologist, I truly believe that the part of therapy that provides the most deep inner healing is the relationship and connection between therapist and client. Research backs this up as, time and again, studies have found this to be true and I base my entire way of being in my therapy room around this and see my clients flourish as a result. How powerful it is to feel truly seen, heard and cared for in all our authenticity and nakedness (metaphorically, of course!). This is something we so rarely allow ourselves to do in life as we carry the masks and cautions our wounds have scarred us with. The gift this brings us, and indeed the therapy process, is deep connection not just with our therapist, but with ourselves. A connection that allows us to understand ourselves in ways we never did before, an awareness that more than anything else brings change and, in turn, peace and contentment. In addition, the connection we feel with our therapist helps us build deeper connection with others in our lives. The process shows us that we are worthy of showing up in all our authenticity, and that taking this risk can be hugely rewarding. So, if you find yourself craving connection, both to others and to yourself, I highly recommend you consider giving yourself the gift of therapy.

PRACTISING MEDITATION AND MINDFULNESS TO CULTIVATE CONNECTION

Suffering is due to our disconnection with the inner soul. Meditation is establishing that connection.
AMIT RAY

Meditation and mindfulness offer us incredible healing benefits, one of which is deep connection.

> *My first introduction to building a meditation and mindfulness practice was when my eldest daughter was 11 months old. As I've shared before, although I absolutely adored my beautiful and very precious baby, and the great joy she brought into my life, my mind felt preoccupied with all of the responsibility and challenges of motherhood. I don't remember how or why I began meditating in this period of my life, but I do remember the huge change it brought. It was as if my eyes were newly opened to the beauty and colours around me. Nature captivated me. Moments of connection with others made my heart feel like it could burst. The stillness and calmness that surrounded my soul felt like true bliss. It was listening to a 21-day meditation challenge by Oprah Winfrey and Deepak Chopra that*

drew me into this world. I listened to their voices every night lying in bed and this meditation practice changed my life.

A number of years later I completed a mindfulness-based stress reduction course and my understanding of, and connection with, mindfulness increased tenfold. I won't lie, the course itself was challenging in ways I had never anticipated, even though guided by the most wonderful soul and a mindfulness teacher I recommend to all my clients, but the benefits and understanding it brought my life were phenomenal, especially when it came to feeling connected to myself, to life, and to everyone around me. I had never before fully grasped how much guidance lives within us when we slow down enough to listen closely to our hearts and souls and inner wisdom, but throughout those eight weeks I began tuning into life and into my body at such a deep level. I began tuning in to my loved ones on a far deeper level too, something that led me to listen more and talk less, and that transformed my understanding of them and their needs, and of how to connect with them much more intimately and authentically. Towards the end of our time together, our mindfulness teacher encouraged us to bring something to class that would forever remind us of the journey we had undertaken together and that would help us to continue to connect with both ourselves and others as deeply as we had over the past eight weeks. As I was shopping that week a gorgeous Himalayan salt candle holder caught my eye and I instantly knew this would be my reminder. That candle holder now sits on my desk and travels to all my healing events with me, and I will forever treasure it, just as I treasure mindfulness and meditation.

An element central to the mindfulness-based stress reduction programme, and one that has been found to significantly soothe our nervous system and our anxiety, improve sleep, relaxation and inner peace, and to connect us deeply with our mind, body and soul, is body scan meditation. While practising this mindfulness exercise, you are guided to focus your attention on your different body parts to anchor your awareness to the present moment and to what is happening for you within. During a body scan meditation, as with any practice that aims to still the mind and invite in calm, you may find your focus beginning to wander. If this occurs, gently and non-judgementally bring your awareness back to the guidance of the exercise, your breath or something in your surroundings that you can anchor your awareness to through your senses. Recently I have been using the mantra 'just be here' time and again to bring me back to the present moment, whether while meditating, practising yoga, drinking cacao, reading or connecting with a loved one, and have been reaping the rewards, so borrow my mantra throughout this healing exercise if you feel drawn towards it, or bring it with you following this exercise for when you need it, as a gift from me to you.

HEALING EXERCISE

When the time feels right, find a distraction-free space you feel comfortable in and settle in for the journey I am about to take you on. Find a position to relax into, whether sitting on a chair, meditation cushion or the ground, or lying on a blanket or mat on the floor. Resist lying on a bed or overly soft surface, as the aim is to stay awake while practising this exercise, rather than drifting off to sleep in a state of bliss (as I have been known to do!). During this exercise, allow yourself to engage as slowly and as patiently as you can, taking your time with each body part before moving on to the next. Bask in the stillness and slowness of this moment and the rewards it will bring.

Let's begin:

As you pause here in this stillness, close your eyes or focus your gaze on a fixed point in front of you. Allow your body to soften into the surface supporting it and your breathing to slow and relax. As you do so, pay attention to how your body responds to this change of pace. Focus your attention on the here and now as you settle in for this beautiful healing journey.

I invite you now to slowly bring your awareness to your feet. As you focus your attention here, begin to observe any sensations you may be experiencing in this part of your body. You may wish to wiggle your toes, feeling them against the fabric of your socks or the surface they rest on, or to remain in stillness. Either way, notice the sensations here as best as you can and when you are ready, begin to imagine breathing down to your feet, as if your breath is travelling to them through your nose, lungs, abdomen, all the way to the bottom of your toes, and when it arrives there, gently back up again through your legs, chest, throat and out through your nose. Take your time here as you engage in this stillness and this process. There is no rush, so just be here in this moment.

When you feel ready, allow your awareness of your feet to dissolve and slowly move your attention to your ankles, pausing here to feel any sensations that may be present for you and to breathe into this part of your body. Allow yourself as much time as you need here, soaking up the stillness and the sensations that arrive.

Next, bring your awareness to your calf muscles and any feelings or sensations that arrive for you here; when you feel ready, with curiosity and wonder, focus your attention on your knees and kneecaps, and then your thighs. Pause here to observe any sensations you may be experiencing in this part of your body, or in your legs. Breathe into your thigh muscles, and then draw your breath back up your body through your lungs and your nose, exhaling deeply. If you notice any discomfort as you focus your awareness on your body, try not to judge this sensation but to stay present with it and simply notice it. Observe how your bodily sensations shift and change from moment to moment. No sensation is permanent, so just observe and bear witness to them, exactly as they are.

On your next out breath, allow your awareness of your legs to dissolve and slowly focus your attention on your pelvis, softening and releasing your body and your muscles as you gently inhale and exhale. Send your breath from your nose, lungs and abdomen down into this area of your body, paying attention to any accompanying sensations, before it returns back towards your lungs and you exhale it through your nostrils. Stay here for as long as you need before moving on. Enjoy the peace and stillness and the relaxation that arrives.

From here focus your attention on your lower back and your belly, allowing yourself to sink into any sensations that may arrive with this attention shift. Pause here, taking in anything that occurs for you in this moment, inviting in stillness and gentle focus. Breathe into this part of your body and as your breath moves back up through your chest, invite your awareness to the middle of your back and your chest, breathing in softly and slowly and allowing any sensations that arrive to be experienced. Pause here in this moment as you connect with your body and the rise and fall of your chest.

Next bring your awareness to your upper back and shoulders, focusing your attention on any sensations that may be present here in a part of your body that does so much for you. Become aware of any sensations in your muscles or any tension that may be present for you. With each out breath, let go of any tension or knots you may be carrying here and if your body feels drawn to doing so, allow your shoulders to drop even more or to sink into the surface supporting them. Send your breath to this part of your body and imagine it reviving you and bringing you any healing that is needed.

On your next out breath, shift your awareness to your arms and any sensations that you may be experiencing here. Remain curious and judgement-free as you rest your attention here, soaking up anything that arrives for you in this moment. Pause here as you breathe and tune in to this moment and to your body. Allow this awareness and focus to now shift to your hands and fingertips. Channel your breathing into and out of this area of your body and if your mind wanders, gently bring your awareness back to the sensations of your hands and fingers and allow yourself to pause here in this moment.

Draw your attention now to your neck and throat region. With curiosity, pause here to discover if any sensations await you. Allow your breath to gently inhale and exhale as you rest your focus here a moment, soaking in whatever is present for you in this part of your body.

On your next exhale, shift your attention to the muscles of your face, allowing them to relax, and focus your awareness on what may be happening in this part of your body, right in this moment. How do the muscles of your face feel? Pay curious attention and rest here awhile as you do so, gently bringing your awareness back to the task at hand if it wanders. Notice the movements of your face as you breathe in and out of your nostrils or mouth. As you exhale, a softening of any tension you are experiencing may occur. Consider this with curiosity and without force, simply paying heed to the present moment and any sensations that arrive or are present.

I now invite you to focus your awareness from the crown of your head all the way down along your body, as you widen your sense of self, all the way to your feet and to the end of your toes. Feel the gentle rise and fall of your chest and the rhythm of your breath as you pause here in this moment, soaking it all in.

As we come to the end of our practice, take a full and healing deep breath, welcoming in the energy of this practice and the abundance of your body. Exhale fully, releasing any tension that you wish to expel, and when you feel ready to do so, open your eyes or lift your gaze from where it was resting and bring your attention back to the space that you are in and to the present moment. Rest here for a while before returning to the outside world, soaking in the relaxation and stillness this wonderful body scan has invited in.

CULTIVATING CONNECTION THROUGH VULNERABILITY AND AUTHENTICITY

Meaningful connection is formed when we bravely share our truth.
MICHELLE MAROS

For years I lived in a bubble of shame. From the moment of my conception I was a secret to hide from the world and from my biological family. I came into the world in this way. Something to be kept quiet and hidden from view until I was handed over to someone else to present to the world. I carried this shame with me as I grew up. It was always in my psyche, always in my subconscious, something I had absorbed in the womb, wrapped up in a dark grey cloud. I felt ashamed when telling new and significant people in my life of the circumstances of my entry into the world, never feeling good enough as a result of my history, often bracing myself for their reaction to my disclosure. Five years ago, after carrying this shame with me for my entire life, I felt compelled to let it go by sharing my story with the world and, in doing so, saying 'This is me. Accept me as I am, in all my wholeness, or turn your back on me. The decision is yours.' With this decision, I spoke up and spoke out and shared my story through connecting with my vulnerability and authenticity and everything I carried within me.

In doing so, two remarkable things happened for me. First, suddenly, as if it were simply time to go, my shame dissipated, vanishing into dust, and offering me a new-found sense of freedom that I had never before experienced. Second, through sharing my vulnerability and authenticity, I connected with the world, and with those who listened to my story, in a way I had never done before. Hundreds and hundreds of people reached out to me in the aftermath and celebrated me and my 'confession', showering me with praise and love and thanking me for my honesty; through listening to my story, many felt compelled and inspired to share their own.

STEP EIGHT CULTIVATE CONNECTION SUMMARY

I share the above story with you to highlight the incredible power of vulnerability and authenticity in achieving connection. True and deep connection is facilitated by opening our hearts and souls to others and, in doing so, allowing them in, as risky as it may feel. For years I stood on the sidelines, too afraid to allow myself to connect and to open myself up fully to others, and so I felt disconnected, isolated and alone. Sharing my vulnerability and authenticity changed everything for me, despite how terrified I was. So if I can offer you one take-away from Step Eight Cultivate Connection, let it be this:

If you feel disconnected, alone or as if you are longing to finally lower your mask and to connect as you never have before, through pausing and listening to the whispers within, through doing 'the work' that I suggest throughout this deeply healing step, and through leaning into your vulnerability, authenticity and inner beauty, you *can* and *will* change your life.

STEP NINE

HONOUR YOUR BOUNDARIES

The more you value yourself,
the healthier your boundaries are.
LORRAINE NILON

For two years I worked with a very special client named Sophie. Sophie was in her early twenties and in that delicious period of life where the hard work of university was over and she was reaping the rewards of a monthly salary that afforded her to move out of home to live with friends, to travel and to party as often as she desired. Sophie was exuberant about this after living with her parents all her life, particularly as her relationship with her mother was very enmeshed (she and her mother had absolutely no boundaries, so their lives were intertwined in a very unhealthy way). What exacerbated this situation was her mother's hidden drinking, and the impact this had had on Sophie's life since she was very young. This created huge fear in Sophie and led her to take on a parentified role; she acted as the parent, berating her mother about her drinking in an attempt to protect her mother's health.

Due to feeling such a lack of control because of this, Sophie initially turned to comfort eating as a little girl, which caused her to gain a significant amount of weight, and then to disordered eating as a teenager, where she lost this weight and became unhealthily thin. Throughout their relationship, Sophie and her mother had zero boundaries. Not only did her mother never set boundaries around things like bedtimes and homework when Sophie was younger, as is so important for a child, but she also frequently criticised Sophie's weight gain and then praised her for her weight loss. This continued even when Sophie's period stopped due to her body being so malnourished, and later in life when Sophie asked her mother to stop commenting on her body.

Alongside working on many other things, Sophie and I focused on her relationship with her mother, especially in relation to introducing and upholding boundaries, and supportive ways Sophie could self-soothe and nurture her inner child when triggered by her mother's comments and hidden drinking. This work was incredibly transformative for Sophie, and hugely changed her relationship with her mother and the boundaries she upheld with herself too. Over the course of two years, Sophie blossomed and changed before my eyes. When I think of her now, as I often do, it is this vibrant young woman who comes to mind.

When I pause to consider boundaries, I think first of the ones I have tried to set with myself:

'Run five kilometres three times a week.'

'Eat less chocolate.'

'Socialise more'.

'Spend less time on your phone and turn it off by 9 p.m.'

As I list them, my mind instantly switches from these desired boundaries to the reality of the situation, which is that for years I almost never managed to maintain them in the way I wanted. When I consider this now, I do so through the lens of knowing that this was largely and most likely due to me setting myself these boundaries out of judgement and the ways I perceived myself to be lacking or not 'enough'.

'Run five kilometres ... to lose weight and tone up.'

'Eat less chocolate ... You eat far too much, you glutton.'

'Socialise more ... You are such a bore and do nothing with your evenings.'

'Spend less time on your phone ... You get distracted so easily and waste so much of your time. What is wrong with you?'

My mind turns too to the times I have tried to introduce and maintain boundaries with others:

'Don't speak to me that way.'

'The one thing I ask of you is that you don't lie to me.'

'Please don't talk about weight in front of my daughter, especially in relation to how big she has got or how heavy she is.'

'I have to leave work by 5 p.m. at the latest.'

However, it is only in recent years that I came to realise that these were often merely requests, rather than boundaries, especially as I would often let them slide or be too fearful to speak up if they were crossed or challenged.

It was my second daughter who taught me the true meaning of boundaries. How clever little ones can be and how much they can teach us. Perhaps this is why parenthood can be so challenging. The best gift in the world but, my God, the hardest! So yes, it was this little being who showed me the true meaning of boundaries and how to actually uphold them. With this new-found knowledge my boundary requests changed from 'Please don't' to 'I can't/I won't let you,' at least when it came to my children:

'I won't let you kick your sister because you might hurt her. We don't kick people, we use our words to express how we are feeling. What would you like to express in this moment?'

'I can't let you go to bed without brushing your teeth. It is my job as your mummy to keep you healthy and safe and to look after you. Brushing your teeth so they don't fall out is a part of that.'

'I can't let you stay up too late, you need your sleep, it helps you to grow and is really important for your health. I know you would like to stay up later tonight, but it's my job as your mummy to look after you, even when that sometimes upsets you.'

Often it is far easier to uphold boundaries with children or those at a lower hierarchical level than us, for example more junior colleagues in work, especially as it can feel extremely intimidating to speak to a partner, peer or authority figure with the language of, 'I can't/won't let you'; however, when we introduce and maintain boundaries with individuals like our partners, peers or authority figures, it is about choosing language that you feel comfortable with that will communicate your boundary in the way that is important to you:

'I'm not prepared to change my mind on this as it is really important to me.'

'I don't know off the top of my head, so I will consider this and come back to you, rather than us finalising it now.'

'That isn't going to work for me, unfortunately, but …'

'I have to leave now but I will come back to you on this tomorrow.'

'I'm not going to stand here and allow you to speak to me in this way. I'm going to leave now and when we both cool down we can continue this conversation.'

The distinction between requests and boundaries is that a request is what you would ideally like from the other, an ask, rather than a rule, whereas a boundary relates to what you are and are not willing to experience, tolerate or accept. A boundary is a limit you put in place to protect yourself. It should be very clear. A request is something that will likely not be viewed with as much consideration, respect or action as a clear-cut and well-presented boundary. Although it does not always feel this way, boundaries do not require permission, justification or explanation, whereas when something is raised in request form (rather than as a boundary) it can often be met with negotiation, a request for compromise, a dismissal or denial.

REFLECTIVE PAUSE

Pause here to consider if you have ever mistakenly voiced requests, rather than boundaries, and if so, if this impacted the outcome of the situation.

If this is something you have indeed experienced, consider too what you could have done differently in the situation to implement and uphold the boundary in the way you desired.

THE ART OF SETTING BOUNDARIES

Love yourself enough to set boundaries. Your time and energy are precious and you get to decide how you use them. You teach people how to treat you by deciding what you will and won't accept.
ANNA TAYLOR

Boundaries are an essential part of maintaining mutually respectful and fulfilling relationships. They protect us and ensure our comfort and safety in our relationships and interactions with others, and make us feel happier and more relaxed, give us a sense of autonomy and control over our lives, and help us to feel more at ease in our sense of psychological safety. When we introduce boundaries, whether with ourselves or others, it is important to first gain clarity on what these boundaries are and why they are important to us. Considering our boundaries in this way will help us uphold them when we set them. Being very clear on what we want and expect in our relationships (including the one we have with ourselves) and being able to revisit our 'why' can be a huge assistance when life gets difficult or when we feel tempted to give up on a boundary or to let it slide 'just this once'.

There are five distinct categories of boundaries:

- physical
- emotional
- intellectual
- sexual
- financial.

So when you consider the boundaries that are important to you, as well as reflecting on your 'whats' and your 'whys', make sure to hold these categories in mind and to distinguish and define the boundaries that fall within each bracket.

REFLECTIVE EXERCISE

Reach for a pen and paper as we pause here to consider our values, needs and desires, and in turn, our boundaries. Do so at a time that feels safe and comfortable, and be gentle with yourself as you engage in this moment.

Part One

The first part in this process is to write a list of your values, so go ahead and do this now, listing as many as you can, before narrowing them down to choose a handful (perhaps five) that most clearly reflect what is important to you.

Learning Note: Values are deeply held beliefs and morals that reflect the worth of something to us and guide our decision making process and how we would like to live our lives.

Examples of values include:

Respect	Reliability
Honesty	Tolerance
Compassion	Peace of mind
Connection	Freedom

Part Two

The next part of this process is to write a list of your needs. Complete this step now, listing as many needs as you can call to mind, before narrowing them down to choose a handful that most reflect where you currently are in your life and what is most important to you.

Learning Note: Over eighty years ago the American psychologist Abraham Maslow created his hierarchy of needs, which highlights the typical needs humans possess in order to live happy and satisfied lives. Within this theoretical model Maslow separates these needs into five categories, beginning with our most basic physiological needs, such as food, water and shelter, before moving on to our need for safety and security, our need for love and belonging, our need for esteem, respect and to feel valued, and, finally, our self-actualising or self-fulfilling needs. Within his hierarchy, Maslow posits that when our basic needs are met, we move our focus to our more advanced needs and set our sights on what comes next in the hierarchy.

Examples of needs include:

Sustenance – food, water, air, sleep, clothing and shelter
A sense of security and safety
Connection
Love
Acceptance
Equality
Justice
Appreciation
Acknowledgement
Respect
A sense of purpose or challenge
Freedom

Part Three
Move on now to writing a list of your desires. List as many desires as come to mind, then narrow them down to a handful that most reflect where you currently are in your life and what is most important to you.

Learning Note: Desires are the things we covet and wish for. These are not essential to our survival or sense of fulfilment in life, and are typically driven by personal preference, trends, marketing campaigns and desire for social status.

Examples of desires include:

Wealth	Material possessions
Adventure	To be desired by others
Travel	Fun
Legacy	Power
Happiness	Fame
Beauty	Success or achievement

Part Four

Using your list of values, needs and desires, call to mind a significant relationship with someone in your life (that someone could include you!) and spend some time considering what your boundaries for this relationship are.

Consider your boundaries during this part of our exercise as a way to care for and protect yourself in this relationship, and make sure to centre them around your values, needs and desires, and the five separate categories of boundaries I define above, as these are all factors that are hugely important to you and your safety, security and happiness levels.

Repeat part four as many times as you feel drawn to when considering the significant people in your life, especially for those of whom you would like to define and introduce new boundaries into your relationship. As this can be a very emotionally evocative exercise, this is a part of our healing process that you can complete now, or one you can return to later on today or tomorrow, when the time feels right. Look after yourself while doing so, and go at a pace that feels right for you.

MAINTAINING BOUNDARIES

Boundaries protect our time and energy, allowing us to focus on what truly matters.

GREG MCKEOWN

Consistency is incredibly important when setting and maintaining boundaries, especially as not consistently upholding boundaries may lead to confusion and a pushing and pulling against them, particularly if the person or persons in question were not happy with their implementation in the first place. For this reason, you will likely need to be assertive and firm about setting your boundaries and in holding firm on the boundaries that are important to you. An essential part of this process will likely be saying 'No', and remembering that '"No" is a complete sentence' (Anne Lamott) and that it is often incredibly important, and indeed necessary, to 'say "No" to make your "Yes's" mean more' (Ana Theus).

When Sophie first began introducing boundaries in her relationship with her mother, it did not go well. Sophie's mother was enraged. How dare her child speak to her in this way after everything she had done for her? Sophie's gentle introduction of healthy boundaries felt like a slap in the face and a huge betrayal, so her mother pushed against them with every fibre of her being. When Sophie asked her to not drink alcohol while she was in the house, her mother stormed out of the room. When she requested her mother didn't comment on her weight or the size of her portions, her mother acted hurt and like she couldn't understand why Sophie would say such a thing. On one occasion, when her mother made disparaging comments about her in front of Sophie's boyfriend and Sophie asked her mother not to speak about her in this way, Sophie's mother laughed and commented, 'Can you believe how sensitive she is, Mark? Our little snowflake.'

This period was incredibly difficult for Sophie because, after all the work we had completed together, Sophie strongly believed she was deserving of the boundaries she was implementing in her life. Because of this new-found strength, and the support our weekly sessions offered her, Sophie worked really hard on remaining consistent in her newly implemented boundaries with her mother, despite the backlash. Eventually, after much self-soothing when things weren't going as swimmingly as Sophie had hoped they would, her mother finally softened to this new dynamic in their relationship. This transformed things for Sophie. She began to enjoy her time at home, and left visits feeling content and planning to return again the following week. Now that her relationship with her mother had changed, she was able to soak up the peace being in her childhood home brought for her and appreciate how easy and relaxing it was to be there.

REFLECTIVE EXERCISE

Reach for a pen and paper and settle in to this moment, allowing yourself to commit to it as deeply as you can.

Begin by pausing to consider your relationship with saying 'No'. Is this something that is familiar to you and that you can do when needs be? Or is it something that feels difficult for you and that you tend to avoid? Spend a moment putting pen to paper as you consider this, for this is incredibly rich and valuable information.

If saying 'No' is indeed difficult for you and something you tend to avoid, what happens for you when you imagine a scenario of saying 'No' to someone?

Tune in to your body as you consider this. Do any emotions, sensations or thoughts arrive for you? For example, do you feel a tightening in your chest or a sense of pressure? Pay attention too to your stomach; does anything happen for you in this area? Do you feel butterflies or the sensation of a knot forming? How are your shoulders feeling in this moment, or the muscles in your face and in your hands? Tune in too to the emotions and thoughts that have arrived for you as you consider this. List these emotions and thoughts on paper, along with the bodily sensations that have come to you.

I invite you now to recall a time where you did say 'No'. Spend some time remembering how this played out and the comfort or discomfort you experienced before, during and after this situation.

When it came to it, how directly were you able to communicate your 'No'? Did it happen as a complete sentence (remember, 'No' can indeed be a sentence in itself), or was your 'No' buried in apologies and justifications. Did you stumble over your words? Document this experience and how you found it. Again, this is rich information for you to build an awareness of, so engage with this as best you can as you pause here in this way.

Thinking about this specific situation, what was the outcome? Was your 'No' respected and heard? Or did the situation result in a different ending? If you think you managed the situation well, spend a moment considering what helped you, as this is really valuable information to take away from this exercise. Alternatively, if you think you could have managed the situation better, or been stronger or clearer in how you voiced your 'No' and upheld it in the aftermath, consider for a few moments what this situation taught you and how you could better navigate a similar situation in the future. Note the thoughts that come to mind for you as you reflect on these questions, and take as long as you need to complete them.

When our boundaries are dismissed, disrespected or crossed, it can feel extremely intimidating to consider how best to navigate this, as there will typically be someone else involved.

The more we practise establishing boundaries with another (or indeed with ourselves) and maintaining them, the more familiar this process will feel and the more at ease we will be. As with all our fears, the more we expose ourselves to them, the more confident we become in our ability to bear whatever we were originally fearful about (whether a fear of dogs, socialising, presenting information at a meeting or driving on a motorway, for example), and the same is true when we establish and maintain boundaries with others, and, indeed, when we are navigating situations in which our boundaries are dismissed, disrespected or crossed.

When this happens and your boundaries are disrespected, it can be incredibly helpful to plan in advance how you will address this. To help with this, I invite you to consider the following model as it can bring structure, a 'how to', and the confidence and assertiveness you will likely need while navigating the crossed boundary.

THE COIN CONVERSATION MODEL

The COIN Conversation Model was developed by Anna Carroll in 2003. It is a simple framework that can be utilised when conversations that you perceive to be difficult or intimidating are required. COIN is an abbreviation of the four steps of the model, which involve:

- **C**ontext

- **O**bservation

- **I**mpact

- and **N**ext Steps of the situation.

The **Context** of the situation is the circumstances or situation you wish to discuss. **Observation** relates to the factual and specific details of what happened. **Impact** focuses on the way the situation has impacted or affected you (and/or others). Finally, **Next Steps** references a clear agreement between you and the other person or people involved in the changes or behaviours needed for you to be able to move on from what happened.

REFLECTIVE EXERCISE

Call to mind a time when a boundary you set was dismissed or crossed by someone in your life. With the COIN conversation model in mind, and following the four steps of the framework, consider how you could have better navigated the aftermath of this situation.

Writing out how you could have discussed each step and your desired outcome with the other person would be a really beneficial way of engaging in this reflective exercise, and of consolidating the learnings of this step, so reach for a pen and paper as you navigate it. Good luck!

BARRIERS TO BOUNDARIES

Daring to set boundaries is about having the courage to love ourselves, even when we risk disappointing others.
BRENÉ BROWN

Maintaining boundaries with yourself can be as difficult, if not even more difficult, than maintaining them with another person. It often takes incredible discipline to honour the boundaries you set for yourself, and let's face it, when implementing new boundaries in your life, you are typically dealing with something you find hard to do! Personal boundaries can link to many areas of your life, for example your finances, your relationships and your sex life, your physical health and your mental health, your relationship with food, your work life and the hours you give to it, and the bad habits you engage in, such as endless scrolling on your phone, drinking too much alcohol or staying up late at night and so depriving yourself of the sleep you need to support you both physically and mentally. Something that can also hugely impact our ability to respect and honour the personal boundaries we set for ourselves is our upbringing and the ways we were taught to sacrifice ourselves and our needs to make others more comfortable. So often we learn early in life to put the needs of others before our own and to respect our elders or important people in our lives, and this can come at a great cost to us, both as children and as adults who carry the legacy of what we were taught in our early lives. We may have also grown up in an environment where boundaries didn't exist or weren't maintained, and so our understanding of boundaries and their importance may be lacking.

> *In 2022 I worked with a client I adored. Nicki was married and had three lovely daughters. She worked part time and looked after her family during the rest of the week, and when she first arrived to our sessions she was absolutely exhausted, overwhelmed and burnt out. Initially Nicki and I worked on regulating her nervous system and for many months I gently encouraged her to begin creating pockets of space for herself (by implementing personal boundaries), even as small as a cup of tea in the morning after the madness of the school run, so she could pause and catch her breath before beginning all of the To Dos her day held in store. It took a great deal for Nicki to become open to looking after herself in this way, and initially she strongly pushed back when I encouraged her to do so:*

> *'I don't have the time, the morning times are so busy for me and if I don't get enough done before lunch, it's no time until the girls are home and I have to look after their every beck and call.'*

'I can't create space for myself at the weekends, I have to taxi the girls around to their matches and parties and activities and John is always off golfing or in the pub.'

'I couldn't possibly go to a weekly yoga class on Tuesday nights, the girls always leave their homework until nighttime and who would help them if I wasn't there? There is always some song and dance about a last-minute home economics project or a hole in their uniform or a school trip that I haven't given permission for.'

When we explored how much Nicki sacrificed herself for her family, I became curious about whether this was something she may have learned while growing up, and indeed it was. Nicki very clearly recalled her mother living her life in exactly the same way, especially as she was bringing up Nicki and her siblings as a single parent. Nicki hugely respected her mother for this and the constant support she provided her family, albeit mainly practical support, rather than emotional, and praised her mother for her work and family ethic and all she did for her family, but when I gently asked Nicki if she would like her own daughters to sacrifice themselves and their needs in this way, Nicki paled and looked as if I had slapped her across the face.

Viewing her behaviour through this lens and the work she and I went on to complete in relation to the cost of her living her life in this way (the cost to her physical health, her mental health, her emotional health, her happiness, her sense of fulfilment and connection – the list goes on) really changed things for Nicki, and she went on to make considerable change in her life, including implementing boundaries with her children and husband and indeed with herself. For example, she set a time every evening when she 'switched off' and if her daughters needed something from her (for example in relation to their homework), they quickly learned to do so before 9 p.m. Likewise, she implemented a boundary with her husband that protected one 'off' evening a week when she could go to the gym or meet a friend, and some sacred 'me time' every weekend too. Nicki also went on to book a girls' weekend away with her schoolfriends, something she would never have allowed herself to do before. She enrolled in a new college course and an eight-week mindfulness-based stress reduction course, which required 40 minutes per day of mindfulness-based meditation. And she even booked a five-night wellness retreat abroad, which she absolutely loved!

As our work together came to a close, Nicki looked and acted like a completely different person from the woman who first sat before me in my therapy room. She was calmer, more regulated, less exhausted, stressed and overwhelmed, and she had a sparkle in her eye and a glow to her skin that I hadn't witnessed before. She was also so full of joy and fulfilment and so looking forward to what the future held for her. The woman who didn't think she could possibly pause for a five-minute cup of tea in the morning had become a happy, carefree and deeply peaceful person. My time with Nicki was a privilege, and incredibly inspiring, both for her three daughters and for me as, through watching Nicki's transformation, we all witnessed the power of boundaries and all that they offered her life.

REFLECTIVE EXERCISE

Before reading on any further, pause here to consider the factors that may prevent you from creating and maintaining boundaries in your life, whether those boundaries are personal in nature, other-focused, or both. Create a list of these factors, and then go back to expand on them one by one to build more awareness of why they may perhaps be blocking your ability to introduce and uphold your boundaries. Allow your inner wisdom to guide you and trust whatever arrives on the page before you.

Other factors that can act as barriers to our boundaries, both our personal boundaries and those we try to implement and uphold with others, are factors such as:

- Guilt
- People-pleasing tendencies
- Fearing rejection
- Low self-worth
- Fear of conflict or confrontation
- Cultural learnings
- Lack of awareness.

Did any of these factors make your list?

BREAKING DOWN BARRIERS TO BOUNDARIES

Boundaries emerge from deep within. They are connected to letting go of guilt and shame, and to changing our beliefs about what we deserve. As our thinking about this becomes clearer, so will our boundaries. Boundaries are also connected to a Higher Timing than our own. We'll set a limit when we're ready, and not a moment before. So will others. There's something magical about reaching that point of becoming ready to set a limit. We know we mean what we say; others take us seriously too. Things change, not because we're controlling others, but because we've changed.

MELODY BEATTIE

Guilt is an emotion I witness all the time in my therapy room and it's something that can absolutely cripple the person experiencing it. As with all our emotions, guilt has a function, and one which is linked to our moral compass, which guides us to live a life that aligns with our values and beliefs. Guilt manifests as 'I have done wrong' (as opposed to shame, which manifests as 'I am wrong' – pause here to revisit Step One Honour Your Emotions for a recap) when we feel we have let ourselves or another down, for example if we lose our temper with someone or feel we have treated them in a way that misaligns with our values; however, guilt can often manifest when it isn't necessarily deserved.

Take my husband, Paul, for example. He often feels huge guilt for making a home for himself two hours away from his parents. Any time something is happening 'up home' and he can't be there, he judges himself. He feels he is letting his parents down and disappointing them. He feels he is not doing his 'duty' as a son. He feels disconnected from them and fears they will perceive him in the way he does himself. However, all these feelings and all this guilt is undeserved; his parents love him dearly, and understand why he chose to build his life where he did. In fact, all they want for him is to be true to himself and to live a happy life, so his guilt is wholly unnecessary and letting go of it would benefit him hugely. (If only he knew someone in his life who could help him with this!)

I imagine you will relate deeply to Paul's story in some way, for we all carry guilt deep inside us. So often I sit with mothers who feel guilty for spending a night away from their children, but as long as our children are safe, time away as parents can be so healthy and can offer us so much. I sit too with people who feel they aren't giving enough to their work when they log off at 5 p.m. (as they are contracted to do!) and there is still work to be done. There will always be work to be done, but rest and relaxation are essential for our wellbeing. Similarly, I often console people who have lost their temper with a loved one and are experiencing huge guilt about it. On these occasions we compassionately look at why they may have lost their temper and use their guilt as hugely valuable information for something they may wish to change in their lives (and with this awareness we can make a plan).

Contrary to belief, guilt isn't a signal that you are 'bad'. Rather it is a message to listen to and, in the first instance, ask, 'Is this deserved? Is this a sign I am living my life misaligned from my values?' If so, then this signal is a real gift, as it can help us to make a change! If not, and if we are able to realise that this guilt is unnecessary and undeserved, then it is time to let it go. Journaling can help with this by reminding yourself of the kind and loving person you are, and how you aren't a 'bad' child, parent, spouse, friend, employee – just one who is doing their best.

REFLECTIVE EXERCISE

In a time and place that you feel comfortable and safe, reach for a pen and paper to complete this reflective exercise. It is one that is particularly important given how often and how easily guilt can prevent us from setting boundaries in our lives, so I strongly encourage you to give as much as you can to it and to do so when you feel you have the time and headspace it (and you) deserve.

To begin, call to mind a time in your life when you experienced significant guilt.

Part A
What happened to cause you this guilt? What was navigating this period like for you? How did you feel while experiencing it? Was this guilt warranted? For example, had you done something that didn't align with your values, or were you beating yourself up over something that was actually okay and healthy for you to do?

Part B
If this guilt was warranted, what could you do differently in the future to help you navigate the circumstances in a way that aligns more with your values? Consider this carefully and write as detailed a response to this question as you can.

If this guilt wasn't warranted, because your behaviour was aligned with your values, spend a moment considering this. Why was this guilt not warranted and why was it appropriate for you to do what you did? For example, were you prioritising your needs in a way that you were deserving of by saying 'No' to something you didn't have the capacity to do?

Put pen to paper to document all of the evidence that points to you not being a 'bad' person who deserved to experience this guilt.

Document also how you can allow yourself to engage in similar future experiences guilt-free and how you can prevent guilt (especially when it is unwarranted) from acting as a barrier to your boundaries.

Guilt can often be a barrier to boundaries if we feel underserving or too guilty to prioritise ourselves and our needs. These beliefs link hugely to our self-worth (as we discussed in Step Seven Strengthen Your Self-Worth), and to lessons and ways of being we were taught in our family of origin – lessons that taught us to prioritise the needs of others ahead of our own. Strengthening our self-worth and silencing our inner critic (as we learned to do in Step Five Silence Your Inner Critic), as well as wrapping ourselves in self-compassion (as we explored in Step Six Cultivate Compassion), will support us along our journey to preventing guilt from persisting as a barrier to honouring our boundaries, as will completing the above reflective exercise as often as you need to and journaling about this emotion and how you can begin to let it go. Working in this way with the familial and cultural learnings we internalised as we grew up will also help us on our journey to honouring the boundaries that are important to us, as we are all so deserving of implementing boundaries in our lives that protect us and keep us safe, physically, mentally and emotionally. I wish you so much luck with bringing change to this barrier to honouring your boundaries, as it is one I work with all the time in my therapy room, and one that is often so unnecessary.

SELF-SOOTHING TO SUPPORT YOUR IMPLEMENTATION OF BOUNDARIES

When we fail to set boundaries and hold people accountable, we feel used and mistreated. This is why we sometimes attack who they are, which is far more hurtful than addressing a behaviour or a choice.
BRENÉ BROWN

> *When things were really difficult in those first few weeks of introducing boundaries with her mother, Sophie relied heavily on the self-soothing techniques she had learned as part of our work together. One of her favourite techniques, that she turned to time and again, was to connect with her inner child to soothe her and, in turn, soothe her adult self. She did this through visualising the little girl inside of her, or through journaling or writing letters to her, and considering what this little girl needed when she felt scared and how Sophie could meet these needs. This often led her to visit beautiful places in nature or ice cream shops!*
>
> *Meditation was part of this process for Sophie too, or brisk walks to release the anxious energy that lingered after difficult conversations with her mother. Sophie found Pilates helpful too and would leave sessions feeling lighter and more relaxed. These processes supported*

Sophie hugely in those challenging weeks and made the transition all the more bearable for her: a transition and a change that benefitted Sophie, and her relationship with her mother, a million times over.

Other factors that can act as barriers to our boundaries are things like a fear of confrontation and conflict, a fear of rejection, and having people-pleasing tendencies. I can deeply relate to all three of these factors because they have most definitely featured in my life and in the past they blocked me from honouring the boundaries I so richly deserve to implement and maintain. Just as the power of strengthening our self-worth, quietening our inner critic and wrapping ourselves in compassion can bring benefits in reducing guilt and our other barriers to our boundaries, these healing processes can also support us in pushing through the fear that may hold us back from voicing our boundaries to others, and indeed maintaining them. Using the techniques we journeyed through as part of Step One Honour Your Emotions, Step Two Calm the Chaos, Step Three Regulate Your Nervous System and Step Four Heal Your Inner Child will also hugely support your ability to honour your boundaries and to brave any difficult conversations or interactions you may have to navigate along your journey towards doing so.

Invite in, too, your somatic techniques; your Worry Time; as many of the healing exercises we have journeyed through that you feel drawn to; your trusty journal; and all you have learned along this healing pathway, just as Sophie did. As part of this process, I share below a deeply powerful healing exercise. It is one that I introduce to many of my clients, and one that has served me well. I hope it brings you as much soothing, comfort and courage as it brings me.

HEALING EXERCISE

I am all too aware that reading about implementing boundaries is one thing, but actually doing the work is another, so allow me to wrap you in a beautiful healing bubble to soothe and calm any fears or anxieties that Step Nine Honour Your Boundaries has brought up for you as we journey towards preparing ourselves to do this work and invest in our happiness, life satisfaction and inner peace. Settle in for this deeply healing experience, making sure you are in a space that feels safe and comfortable for you, and enjoy the ride.

Begin by tuning into your breath and the rise and fall of your chest, taking slow and steady deep breaths in and out. Fall into a rhythm that feels natural for you and as you tune in to your breath and the stillness pausing in this way brings, notice how your body is responding to this nurturing way of being. All you have to do in this moment is breathe. Everything else can wait, this is your time, and your gift to yourself, so if you notice your mind beginning to drift off, gently return your awareness to your breath and the rise and fall of your chest, and if you would like an extra anchor in this moment, place one hand on your belly and the other on your heart, and connect in with the gentle movement of your body.

Allow me now to bring you on a journey that will calm your body, heart and soul, soothe your mind and prepare you to speak your boundaries and your truth with confidence and grace.

Picture yourself in a tranquil and picturesque place, a place where you feel at peace and relaxed. Here, you have no cares in the world and nothing to do in this moment except be. Trust what has arrived for you in this moment, allowing yourself to drop into this space through your senses, soaking in the smells, the temperature on your skin, the touch beneath your feet, the sounds, and anything that catches your eye. Drink in the beauty of this space and soak in how it is making you feel, just by being here. Rest here awhile, for you are tired and this peaceful healing space is such a joy to behold.

I invite you now, in your special and safe place, to visualise the arrival of a bright bubble; one you feel incredibly drawn to wrapping yourself in. This bubble is inviting, healing, sparkling, and calling to you. It is one you know that is just for you and that is sent to protect you and fill you up with everything you need. Step into this bubble and allow it to embrace you in its peace and warmth and light. It feels so wonderful to sink into the love and energy this bubble possesses and you feel so safe and so supported here. Rest here for a while, enjoying the peace and stillness, filling up your cup with everything that is flowing from this beautiful bubble to you.

When you are ready, I invite you to bring to mind someone who has caused you distress at some point your life. Someone who has challenged you, someone who has made you feel sadness or pain or maybe even fear. Someone who has not always respected you or treated you in the way that you wished for, in the way that you deserve. They may have hurt you deeply, or it may be someone you love dearly who made a mistake or lost their temper and hurt you in the process. This person might be a family member, a partner, a friend, an authority figure ... allow whoever comes to mind to arrive into your thoughts. You are safe in your bubble and they cannot harm you, whatever they may have done or said in the past.

I invite you now to transport yourself in your protective, light-filled bubble from your deeply healing special place to an environment where you would like to meet this person. Take your time to visualise this, as best you can, arriving in this environment in the safety of your bubble.

When you feel ready, invite this person to arrive into this moment with you. As you do so, you can see them clearly from your bubble, something that feels so protective for you because you know they cannot penetrate it; in fact, they cannot even see it. It is as though you are watching them from a very special cocoon, without them having any awareness that it is surrounding you.

As you acclimatise to this new environment and the person before you, you see them exactly as they are and you realise as you watch them that your healing bubble is filling you with self-worth, self-love and self-respect, as well as courage and a fire in your belly, a fire that leads you to feel brave and courageous and as if you have the power to do anything in this moment, even to have a difficult conversation or encounter you once may have shied away from or avoided. You consider this person before you, and the way they have hurt you in the past, and you feel so ready to implement a new boundary with them, one that is important to you, one they will respect and honour, because deep down in your heart, you see so clearly how worthy you are of this.

As the warmth and light from your beautiful bubble surrounds you, send yourself love as you prepare to set this boundary. You feel so safe in your protective bubble and ready to speak your truth and to share what you need to from the heart. You feel so full of self-love and worthiness and with these emotions and feelings supporting you, you take a deep breath and begin to share your boundary with the person before you and whatever it is you need to get off your chest. Go ahead and do so now, saying as much as you need to and taking as much time as you need, with the light and protection of your bubble surrounding you.

Once you have shared everything with them, you watch them as they soak in your words. They may react to what you have said.

If they do, their words don't flood you or make you feel the way you typically would in this scenario. Their words merely bounce off your bubble and reflect back to them, so their energy cannot hurt you or penetrate your bubble. You feel a new awareness in this moment, one that is deep within your heart, that their reaction is theirs and that it has nothing to do with you; rather, it relates to how they feel about themselves and the world around them. You realise this deeply now as you watch them from the safety of your bubble.

With this new awareness you realise too that you perceive their words and actions differently now. You can see them for who they are. Perhaps it's their desire to feel in control or to avoid losing you. Perhaps it's fear. Perhaps it's that they feel threatened or intimidated. Perhaps it's something they learned from their parents. Whatever it is, your new-found awareness softens their words and their behaviours and you may even start to view them with compassion and understanding as you watch them with this new sense of their vulnerability and fallibility.

After they have done or said whatever it was they felt they needed to, they come to a halt before you, and you both spend a moment in silence together, feeling that everything that needed to be said has been said and that you can both rest now in this moment, side by side. Enjoy this moment of stillness, enjoy having had the courage to share yourself in this way with them, and enjoy the warmth and safety of your bubble as you rest here for a while.

When you feel ready, say your goodbyes and begin your journey back to your special place, leaving this person and the space you were in.

As you arrive back at your peaceful and tranquil place you feel so happy with yourself and so calm. Saying everything you needed to has been so freeing, and you relish this as you rest in your special place, soaking in the sights, the sounds, the sensations and the wonderful energy that surrounds you. Rest here for as long as you need to as you fill up your cup and nourish yourself.

As you begin to feel ready to leave your beautiful bubble and this incredibly special place, remember that you can return here any time you need to or want to. Likewise, remember that you can call on your bubble whenever you need it, and wrap yourself up in its safety where the reactions and words of others will not be able to penetrate you or burden you. Your bubble will always be waiting for you. It is something you can wrap yourself up in every single day as you navigate life and all that it brings. In fact, if you would like to bring it back to the outer world with you, you absolutely can. The choice is yours. You are free to journey back to the outer world in whatever way you wish.

When you are ready, bring your awareness back to your breath and the rise and fall of your chest. Slowly bring some movement into your fingers and your toes and gently stretch and shift any parts of your body that you feel called to. When you are ready, open your eyes, slowly and gently taking in your surroundings, before returning to your day renewed and with a new-found sense of confidence, self-awareness, self-love and self-worth.

After engaging in this healing exercise, take as long as you need before reading on. You have all the time in the world. This experience shouldn't be rushed, so take it at a pace that feels gentle and right for you.

REFLECTIVE EXERCISE

Before Step Nine Honour Your Boundaries comes to a close, I invite you to pause to complete one final reflective exercise. Reach for a pen and paper – writing down what comes to mind for you as part of this process will offer you the opportunity to connect deeply with this pause and the wisdom you hold within.

As Brené Brown says, 'When we fail to set boundaries and hold people accountable, we feel used and mistreated', and so often we can experience resentment, frustration and disappointment. This is a natural response to feeling stretched, disrespected, taken for advantage and the many other feelings and emotions that can arise for us when we fail to honour and maintain our boundaries.

Pause here to consider a time you felt this way.

Outline the situation and how it made you feel.

What thoughts, emotions and bodily sensations did you experience during this situation?

How did you behave while navigating it?

Did you do or say anything you later regretted?

With all the knowledge you have gained throughout Step Nine Honour Your Boundaries, and with the gift of hindsight, how could you have navigated this experience better?

If something like this were to happen in the future, how would you like to navigate it?

Take as long as you need here to consider this reflective exercise, and allow and welcome in the emotions and experiences that arrive for you as you to do. Be gentle with yourself throughout this process, and if it feels emotive and difficult in any way for you, consider what you need in the moment to support you throughout it or, indeed, in the aftermath.

STEP NINE HONOUR YOUR BOUNDARIES SUMMARY

There is a beautiful process that happens with every single client I sit with. Usually they enter our relationship apologetic for their needs, apologetic for their struggles, apologetic for the emotions that flow, almost as if they are apologetic for taking up the space between us. However, as they ease into our work and learn that it is safe and valid (not to mention healthy!) to voice and express themselves in all their authenticity, they begin to believe in themselves … in their power. In their worth. In how deserving they are of looking after and nurturing themselves, and of showing up in the world in whatever way feels meaningful and true to them. With this new way of being comes boundaries. And 'Nos'. And permission to honour, respect and protect themselves. This shift that I observe in every single client is powerful and life-changing and it is a shift that can be seen in them physically too. They hold themselves differently. They no longer lower their gaze. They shine. This is the transformation that self-worth and permission to honour and uphold your boundaries brings into your life, so thank you for journeying through Step Nine Honour Your Boundaries with me. I hope that by soaking in the above wisdom you too begin to transform into someone who honours and upholds the boundaries you are so deserving of, and as you move on to our final step, Step Ten Accept What Is, you do so with a new-found knowledge and confidence, and an excitement for what lies ahead.

STEP TEN

ACCEPT WHAT IS

The two parts of genuine acceptance – seeing clearly and holding our experience with compassion – are as interdependent as the two wings of a great bird. Together, they enable us to fly and be free.
TARA BRACH

A number of years ago I went through a really challenging conflict in my life. It was something I never anticipated would happen to me. You hear these stories and listen to them, intrigued, perhaps passing judgement or wondering how the situation or conflict came to be, but never thinking it could one day happen to you. This was my situation, and one I struggled with immeasurably. It knocked me in every way it could and brought out all my insecurities and vulnerabilities. I doubted myself as never before, wondering, 'Am I the person this situation and conflict is suggesting? Am I callous and thoughtless and unkind?' I had never before considered myself in these ways, but the experience I was going through had me wondering if I was as bad a person as this situation was hinting at. I cried so much that year, often in bed at night, flooded with the emotions I avoided during the busyness of my day. It was so painful to think about that I did everything I could not to, but a pot of water always boils if there is enough intensity in the flame.

With this conflict I cocooned myself from the world. Life felt safer that way and when your mind is so full of pain and self-doubt, exhaustion will eventually take over. For the guts of a year, if not longer, I avoided doing certain things and seeing certain people. My nervous system just wouldn't allow it. I was far too anxious and on such high alert that even thinking of putting myself into certain environments (ones specific to the situation and the people involved) was too much for me. I knew this was happening; it was a conscious decision, not an unconscious one that was playing out unbeknownst to me, but when in survival mode you do all you can to protect yourself, and survival mode I was most definitely in.

During this time, I also avoided doing all the things I would usually lean on to support me with my emotions. For example, I point blank refused to journal. I just couldn't. Putting pen to paper and admitting the seriousness of it all was too much for me. It would break me. I didn't have it in me. So I didn't. However, this meant I bottled up all the emotions inside me (hence the emotional flooding at night and the sleep that eluded me as my mind combusted). I did speak about it to a few trusted people, and that was helpful, but I didn't accept their compassion and kindness, instead thinking, 'They are just being nice and have to say these things.' The inner critic in me led me to wonder and, more often than not, believe that I was the one to blame and in 'the wrong' for what was happening in my life. I was experiencing a process that I saw so frequently in my clients, self-doubt and self-berating when challenge arose, and taking on full responsibility despite it never solely being one person in the wrong – it takes two to tango, after all. Sometimes anger would arise in me, 'I don't deserve this. I haven't done something to warrant the intensity of the situation and the words and actions of others.' In these moments my fleeting self-worth paid a brief visit before eluding me again, at which I would return to thoughts of 'Am I a bad person? Do I deserve to be treated in this way? Have I brought this on myself?'

This cycle continued for months, until eventually I came to a place where I was ready to process what was happening. I say 'I was ready', but really the Universe forced it upon me. Life has a funny way of doing that, doesn't it? This 'force' was via a wellness retreat I was attending that felt like the start of a new chapter, where I was moving on from the situation that had been weighing me down for so long. Instead of a fresh start and a new chapter, however, I found myself feeling as if I was right back at the start of my emotional processing of the situation. (I had never truly allowed myself to sit with and feel the emotions I was experiencing and carrying.) I fell apart that week. I sobbed and sobbed and sobbed and allowed those around me to hold me. I went to Reiki and ancestral healing sessions, and opened myself up to receiving whatever healing support I needed. I was so lovingly held by everyone on the retreat that week that something really powerful happened for me. I saw my pureness, my kind heart and my warm soul, and I just knew that the dark thoughts I had been carrying for so long weren't true. I wasn't a 'bad person'. I hadn't done something despicable and shameful and horrendous. I wasn't the person I questioned myself to be in those darkness, tear-filled moments.

This emotional release and surrender shifted things for me hugely that week and on leaving that retreat I could see that what had occurred was due to pain. Deep, unprocessed pain that people were carrying. Deep, unprocessed pain and shame and loss. With this awareness came acceptance. I could consider my own dance moves in the tango, and the actions I took and whether I could have done or said or acted differently, but I could never do that for another person or change how they were feeling. That responsibility was theirs and all I could do was work on myself and my own healing. With that acceptance, and the acceptance of what was, came a new sense of freedom that I had never before experienced, and a deep sense of compassion. 'It's okay that you have really struggled with this. You are only human and to be human is to struggle. What do you need in this moment to look after yourself and to continue on, despite this weight being present in your life?'

SO WHAT DOES ACCEPTANCE ACTUALLY MEAN?

Acceptance involves the action of allowing the presence of all experiences – internal and external, positive and negative – as they are in the moment, without attempting to change the form or frequency of these experiences.
JILL A. STODDARD AND NILOOFAR AFARI

Acceptance is the process of allowing things to be, just as they are, without trying to change them. Acceptance calls for openness, receptibility and flexibility. Pushing against these often causes us to struggle in our lives, exactly as I did in my shared story, for I completely refused to accept and sit with my emotions and in what was happening in my life, or to place myself in situations where I could be faced with the experience and struggle I was dealing with. I also deeply personalised and blamed myself for what was happening in a very childlike manner because, as we mentioned in Step Four Heal Your Inner Child, developmentally a young child has a very egocentric view of the world, believing that everything that happens in their immediate environment is wholly linked to them, their behaviours and their worth. And I was most definitely responding from the inner child deep inside of me throughout this incredibly painful experience.

A central part of acceptance is that our efforts to change or manipulate situations or unwanted or painful experiences are often the main cause of the psychological and emotional pain we may experience while enduring them. Acceptance typically allows us to engage in more supportive and meaningful behaviours and to live a more full and free life (exactly what my eventual acceptance of the above situation led me to). The concept of acceptance has been widely studied in the field of psychology, especially due to its link to acceptance and commitment therapy, an evidence-based therapy modality that aims to support individuals to manage difficult sensations, feelings, thoughts and circumstances. This research has found that through welcoming in and working towards acceptance, or the idea of making space for or opening up to something that is happening without attempting to remove, alter, control or resist it helps to lower the impact on us of unpleasant or distressing emotions and circumstances. Practising acceptance has been found to alleviate stress, pain (both physical and emotional), depression, anxiety, eating disorder behaviours, self-harm and suicidal ideation, and addiction, and to improve emotional well-being and quality of life, increase resilience and emotion regulation, and develop psychological and emotional awareness. Acceptance is not a practice that people typically find easy; in fact, it can be quite the opposite in that individuals often push and rebel against it, because the struggle associated with the experience or circumstance can be incredibly painful. However like almost every concept I have introduced you to throughout our ten-step healing journey, acceptance can be practised and worked towards, and when developed as a skill it can become much easier to achieve and, most importantly, maintain.

It is vital to note that acceptance is not the same as forgiveness. In fact, although the word 'forgiveness' is frequently thrown about in relation to therapy, it is not always possible or appropriate to aim for. For example, if someone did something absolutely horrendous to you (I'm talking worst nightmare scenario), would it be absolutely necessary or appropriate to forgive them as part of your healing journey? Perhaps acceptance of what has happened is the more appropriate process to work towards, especially if something cannot be changed or 'fixed'. Often forgiveness is suggested as a way to 'let go' and move on, and to release anger someone may be carrying in relation to an experience they have undergone or are holding on to, especially if it would benefit that person for their relationship with the other to be repaired. However, acceptance alone can offer a sense of letting go and moving on, and deep emotional processing and release. Forgiveness involves letting go of resentment, blame and anger and extending kindness to the other in the form of compassion and understanding; while acceptance involves the act of offering that kindness, compassion and understanding *to yourself*.

In my therapy room, the topics that arrive most commonly while working towards acceptance are:

- Acceptance of themselves and the parts of them that they have pushed against.

- Acceptance of a loss, be it the loss of a loved one through death or the ending of a relationship, or the loss of a part of their identity or something they have held dear to them that is no longer possible or available.

- Acceptance of their parents or a significant other in their life, due to their behaviour or a way they have let them down, whether intentional or due to a lack of capacity or understanding.

- Acceptance of something that has happened, whether through their own fault or another's, or something that could not have been escaped or avoided.

- Acceptance of something that is extremely challenging to bear psychologically, such as a health diagnosis, trauma, betrayal, rejection or significant criticism.

- Acceptance of not being able to control things, especially others.

- Acceptance of significant change.

- Acceptance of the past.

- Acceptance of needing help.

HEALING EXERCISE

Complete this exercise in a space that is comfortable and distraction-free, and at a time when you will not feel the need to rush, and when you feel ready to engage in a deeply healing exercise, but one that may bring up some emotion for you. When I am preparing to complete healing exercises such as the one I am sharing with you now, I often dim the lighting and burn candles, essential oils or incense, as I feel these support my senses and ability to relax into the task. I also ensure that I am warm and cosy, and may play soothing music or wrap up in my favourite blanket on the couch.

To begin this healing exercise I invite you to spend a moment (or as long as you need) searching for a time when you felt strong emotion. Allow yourself to call in this emotion and the related situation as vividly as you can and in as much detail as feels comfortable for you, perhaps closing your eyes and focusing your attention as best you can on whatever is arriving for you. Don't force it; simply invite in the thoughts, emotions and sensations and pay attention to what happens for you in doing so. Be as curious and as open to this experience as possible – it is in the arrival and feeling of these emotions and thoughts that the healing comes. Pause here to connect as vividly as you can with what arrives for you.

As you pause, pay attention to how you are experiencing what I am inviting you to do. Often we have preconceptions of what connecting with our emotions will be like, but the experience is not as daunting as we expect. Be gentle and non-judgemental with yourself as you complete this exercise. If you *are* finding it difficult, that is a welcome and very human way to be.

As you call in this experience, pay attention to what is happening for you in your body and any sensations you may be experiencing. If any sensations arrive, lean into them and try as best you can to identify where you are experiencing them in your body. Allow yourself to simply pay heed to them and their arrival, rather than trying to block them or resist them. These sensations, and any thoughts or emotions that arrive with them, are messages to you and ones that are full of information and value. How do these sensations feel? What shape or form do they take? Are they heavy, static or moving? Are they exerting a pressure on you or do they feel that they are weighing you down? If I were to ask you to describe them to me, what words would you put on them? Be gentle as you consider these questions and tune in to how you are feeling. Take things slowly and be kind to yourself.

As you engage in this healing exercise, pay attention to any judgemental thoughts that arrive for you. If your inner critic or inner judge decides to pay a visit with comments such as 'This is too hard, I don't want to do this' or 'You are so weak for struggling with this,' don't take them at face value or attach meaning and truth to them. Instead, take a step back and merely consider these thoughts and why you may be having them in this moment. Welcome them with curiosity and an open mind. They are just thoughts, and not all our thoughts are true; some are merely judgements with no factual evidence behind them, and ways our mind tries to trick us or protect us. Also bear in mind that you are viewing these thoughts, if you are experiencing them, through an emotional lens, so rather than making meaning of them, try, as best you can, to observe them from a distance. That will take away their 'bite' and their power.

Focus now as best you can on the original emotions and situation that arrived for you when you first began this exercise. The original emotion and situation that brought struggle and suffering into your life. As you focus on these emotions and associated thoughts and bodily sensations, try to do so with a sense of gentleness and compassion. If you are finding this experience difficult, accept this as best you can; 'I am finding this exercise difficult and emotive but I can bear this discomfort and I know it is only temporary.' Accepting this discomfort is not about forcing yourself to 'like' the experience, or to find it any less distressing, but about allowing and welcoming in however you are feeling and sitting with it as best you can as a way to process, release and heal your internal world.

As you experience these emotions and this struggle, can you connect with it in the same way you would connect with the suffering of another? Can you offer yourself the same compassion, softness and patience you would offer someone else navigating this experience? Can you hold yourself in this kindness, love and care? Pause here for a moment to consider this, and if you feel able to, to offer yourself this compassion, softness and patience.

As you engage in this healing exercise, I invite you to begin naming each of the emotions you are experiencing, for example 'that's fear', 'that's sadness', 'that's anger'. As you connect with these emotions, do so with compassion and acceptance; 'It is hard to feel this, and very painful, I am sorry you are experiencing this pain right now, I'm here with you,' as if you are connecting with the part of you that is finding this healing exercise really difficult, the part of you that needs some tender loving care. As you offer yourself this compassion, allow the words of support to sink into your body and to embrace you and your struggle.

To further support yourself in this moment, consider placing one or both of your hands on the areas of your body that are feeling the most heightened or where you are feeling the deepest bodily sensations. Lovingly support this part of your body as you connect with it and visualise, as best you can, sending it love and comfort. This could take the form of imagining that you are sending it a white healing light or wrapping it in soothing blue healing waters. Imagine this comfort and love flowing from your hands to this part of your body and lovingly surrounding this area with a warm embrace. Remember, you aren't attempting to change or alter how you are feeling in this moment, rather you are working towards accepting and comforting yourself in what has arrived for you, as you navigate the emotional experience you are undergoing. Stay here in this moment for as long as you need, feeling all that has arrived for you, and meeting it with patience, love and kindness. Sit with your internal experience and trust that in doing so you are healing the pain you carry and offering yourself exactly what you need in this moment.

When you are ready to move away from this moment, and to part ways with the emotions and distress you have been bearing witness to, I invite you to gently bring your focus to your breath, connecting with the rhythm of your body and the rise and fall of your chest. As you breathe, I invite you to complete one last scan of your body and if there is any remaining tension or difficult sensation present, I encourage you to breathe into this, asking your body to release the struggle it is experiencing in relation to what you are carrying, and to instead allow it to be there, exactly as it is. Take as long as you need and when you feel ready, introduce some gentle movement into your body, perhaps wiggling your fingers and toes, and slowly opening your eyes and taking in, little by little, the environment you are in.

As you return fully to the external world, I invite you to take a moment to thank yourself for engaging in this healing exercise and connecting with and accepting your most uncomfortable emotions, thoughts and bodily sensations, and offering yourself compassion, comfort and acceptance while doing so. As you bring this healing exercise to a close, I invite you to spend a moment reflecting upon and journaling what this exercise was like for you. There is no right or wrong here, simply an exploration of the experience and how you found it, so welcome whatever arrives on the page, and when you have finished, pause a moment to consider how you can look after yourself in the aftermath of this exercise and for the remainder of the day.

WHAT ACCEPTANCE ISN'T

Acceptance doesn't, by any stretch of the imagination, mean passive resignation. Quite the opposite. It takes a huge amount of fortitude and motivation to accept what is – especially when you don't like it – and then work wisely and effectively as best you possibly can with the circumstances you find yourself in and with the resources at your disposal, both inner and outer, to mitigate, heal, redirect, and change what can be changed.

JON KABAT ZINN

To consider acceptance from another perspective, let's first consider what it is not. Acceptance is not agreeing with something. Acceptance is not resignation. Acceptance is not approving of or condoning someone else's poor behaviour. Acceptance is not 'giving up'. Acceptance is not trying to predict what may happen in the future and so taking an action or feeling a certain way. It is about staying present with what is happening in the here and the now, without resisting it or trying to change it, and worrying about the future when the future arrives. So often, in antithesis to working towards acceptance, we suppress. Our emotions. Our feelings. Ourselves. But where does this suppression get us? Nowhere!

I recently worked with Lauren, a bubbly, optimistic, funny, matter-of-fact woman, who it was an absolute joy to support throughout the ups and downs of her life. Lauren was married, and a mother, and her own mother featured very heavily in her life. This was important for Lauren, for she felt a deep sense of responsibility to be there for her, but it was also a huge bone of contention in her life, because at times Lauren wished her mother could be there for her, rather than her mother and their relationship being Lauren's responsibility. When we initially began exploring the feelings Lauren had about her mother, although she loved her dearly, she experienced and expressed a lot of anger:

'How can she not see how much she leans on me and depends on me? And how does she not realise that I need support too? It's not supposed to be a one-way thing.'

'How can she think it's okay to contact me so much, even when I'm at work? I've started screening her calls because I just can't cope with the constant intrusion in my life where she expects me to attend to her every need, most of which are completely superficial.'

'I am finding this struggle I'm experiencing really difficult and lonely. I wish my mum could support me in matters like these, especially emotional ones, but she just doesn't get it and often just brings the subject back to herself.'

For months Lauren expressed her frustration during our therapy sessions and at times tried to speak to her mother in a very gentle way about how she was feeling. However, it felt as though these conversations always fell on deaf ears; or if her mother did hear what Lauren was trying to communicate with her, she would become wounded very quickly and very deeply, which would lead to Lauren feeling guilty for even bringing it up, and, ultimately, even more frustrated.

We worked on acceptance a lot throughout our time together in my therapy room. Accepting her mother for the person she was. Accepting their relationship despite the dynamics that it had. Accepting her mother's constant desire for connection and support, and as a result her frequent calls and interruptions in Lauren's life. Accepting her mother despite her inability to support Lauren emotionally in the way that she was yearning for (and likely had been yearning for her entire life). As part of this process Lauren sat with all of the emotions that flooded her. The sadness and loss because her mother couldn't show up for her in the way she desired. The anger she felt when she saw yet another call from her mother flashing on her phone. The guilt she experienced when she expressed how she was feeling to her mother, only to be met with stone-walling and passive aggression. Lauren welcomed these emotions, allowing them to circle her. She didn't try to resist them or suppress them or deny them; she simply accepted them as they were while compassionately supporting herself through the process and the emotional release. It got to a stage where Lauren no longer tried to change her mother or their relationship, but simply realised that by accepting her, warts and all, she would feel less frustrated and less like she was punching a brick wall.

With this acceptance came the realisation that Lauren had other people in her life who could support her on the emotional level she was seeking: me and our work together; her husband; her best friend; a colleague she had worked with for years who was wise and patient and always there for her. This realisation would not have come for Lauren if she had kept punching that brick wall, and neither would the freedom that arrived for her in the pausing and sitting with what was, despite the pain of it and the tears that flowed alongside that pain. Lauren realised during all of the hard work she engaged in that she would never have the mother she fantasised about, but while navigating the process she developed the resilience she needed to accept that. In doing so, she was able to see the support and love that was there for her, including from her mother, just in different ways from those she had hoped for.

REFLECTIVE PAUSE

Can you relate to Lauren's story? Has there ever been a person or situation in your life that you fantasised and wished could be different? If so, consider this situation for a moment and how it impacted you. Bring this to mind as vividly as you can, taking your time to allow yourself to connect with this reflective pause as best you can. While doing so, as part of the process, consider too your thoughts, emotions, behaviours and bodily sensations at the time of the experience.

Consider also whether you were pushing and pulling against what was; or hoping things could be different and perhaps even trying to manipulate things so they could be? Again, pause as part of the process to really consider the impact navigating this experience had on you.

Finally, like Lauren, were you able to move towards a place of acceptance with this? Or is it still a work in progress for you?

There is no right or wrong here, and your answers are for you only, so be as honest with yourself as you can.

Pause here to consider these questions as fully as you can.

SELF-ACCEPTANCE

The most terrifying thing is to accept oneself completely.
CARL JUNG

We discussed above that acceptance is the process of allowing things to be, simply as they are, without trying to change them. The same is true of self-acceptance. The aim of this process is to accept ourselves completely, exactly as we are.

Self-acceptance embraces us in our entirety, without conditions or exceptions. Self-acceptance holds us in both the parts of ourselves that we welcome and celebrate, as well as those darker shadow parts of ourselves that we sometimes feel urged to hide or to dismiss or to suppress.

Self-acceptance, like acceptance in general, is hard-earned and very rarely easy to embrace. It is a practice and a process and something we typically must work hard for, but when achieved, it is truly transformative. Self-acceptance links to the worth we place on ourselves. So often we attribute our worth to our external appearance, what we have to offer others around us, or our achievements in life, but as we learned in Step Seven Strengthen Your Self-Worth, self-worth is an internal core belief of being of value and 'good enough'. Good enough and worthy of love, good enough and worthy of all of the wonderful things that happen in our lives, good enough and worthy to exist and take up space in the world, irrespective of external factors, such as our appearance, success or achievements. This can link strongly to the strive for perfection I so often witness in my therapy room, and indeed in myself; however, striving for perfection (a concept that doesn't actually exist, and so, is never in fact achievable) isn't really centred on an aim to do things perfectly, but rather is the process of finding faults easily. Read that again: perfection isn't really centred on an aim to do things perfectly, but rather is the process of finding faults easily.

It's powerful when considered in this way, isn't it?

In Step Six Cultivate Compassion, we worked towards embracing ourselves exactly as we are with kindness, patience and understanding, and self-compassion is a huge component of acceptance (and of self-acceptance). As humans we struggle and suffer, and are, by our very nature, infallible and perfectly imperfect, something we must recognise and embrace if we are to fully embrace and accept ourselves and our lives as they (and we) are. This extends too to the shame and regret we carry in life, and it is through meeting these parts of ourselves and our past mistakes with self-compassion that self-acceptance can bloom. It may be as simple as saying the following to yourself (and repeating it and reminding yourself of it as frequently as you need to until it eventually sinks in):

'I accept all parts of myself and my past in its entirety. I am a fallible human being who has not always taken the correct steps, but these diversions have taught me important lessons, without which I would not be the person I am today.'

Self-acceptance has for me been a long-term work in progress and, if I'm completely honest, something I imagine will be a lifelong journey for me (as deep inner healing often truly is). For many years I pushed and pulled against many parts of myself. My skin colour. My weight. My muscle tone. My wittiness. Growing up, if someone had given me a magic wand and gifted me the opportunity to change myself in whatever way my heart desired, I'm not confident much of my original self would have remained. Isn't that so incredibly sad? How heartbroken I would be if any of my daughters were ever to change any part of themselves – I love them so wholly and completely exactly as they are – yet I wished this for myself on many occasions. The same applies to my dear friends. I have no doubt if given a magic wand they would use it, yet I would deeply miss any part of themselves they changed. If only we could innately view and accept ourselves as fully as we do for others. This may not come naturally, but it is something we can work towards, I promise you.

When it comes to self-acceptance (and, indeed, acceptance in general), the freedom the process can provide (not just arriving at the destination, but the process in itself) is monumental. The calm and inner peace that comes as part of this work is life-changing and can reduce so powerfully the inner struggle and judgement we so often experience. Including this step as part of our ten-step healing journey was something I absolutely had to do, and one I know deep in my heart will bring huge change and comfort to your life if you engage with this process as wholly and fully as I urge you to. For this is the work. This is the healing. This is where the magic happens. Earlier steps in our healing journey will assist us with this, such as our cultivation of compassion, our quietening of our inner critic, our strengthening of our self-worth, our honouring of our emotions and our healing of our inner child. Every step of this ten-step healing journey links together, and the process is incredibly powerful in its entirety if can allow yourself the gift of truly immersing yourself in it.

HEALING EXERCISE

Allow yourself to settle into this moment as fully and as deeply as you can. This is your time and there is nothing for you to do except to be here in this moment.

Sink into the surface supporting your body, whether you are sitting or lying down, and allow yourself to get as comfortable as possible and to melt into this moment. Close your eyes and tune in now to your breath and the rise and fall of your chest. Allow yourself to rest here in this stillness, enjoying the sensations that arise for you as you allow your body, mind and soul to pause in a way we so rarely allow ourselves to do.

As you feel your body beginning to relax, imagine yourself walking on a path through a beautiful forest. With each step you take you feel the softness of the forest path beneath your feet, a mixture of soil, fallen leaves, pine needles and moss. As you walk, your body relaxes and your mind clears more and more with each step you take. Breathe in the fresh forest air, filling your lungs completely. Now exhale, breathing out all of the air in your lungs, letting go of all the stress and tension you have been carrying. Take another deep breath in, hold, and now breathe out again completely. Continue to breathe slowly and deeply as you walk through this peaceful forest.

You notice, as you continue your journey, that the air is warm and comfortable on your skin and you soak up this feeling. Sun filters through the trees, making a dappled pattern on the ground before you. Listen to the sounds of the forest with each step you take. Birds singing. A gentle breeze blowing. The leaves on the trees as they shift and sway in the soft wind. Your body relaxes more and more as you walk. Count your steps and breathe in unison with your strides:

Breathe in, 2, 3, 4 . . . hold, 2, 3, 4 . . . exhale, 2, 3, 4.

Breathe in, 2, 3, 4 . . . hold, 2, 3, 4 . . . exhale, 2, 3, 4.

Breathe in, 2, 3, 4 . . . hold, 2, 3, 4 . . . exhale, 2, 3, 4.

Breathe in, 2, 3, 4 . . . hold, 2, 3, 4 . . . exhale, 2, 3, 4.

As you walk deeper into the forest, feel your muscles relaxing and lengthening. With each stride you take your arms swing gently in rhythm with your steps and your back softens as your spine lengthens and the muscles release. Feel the tension leaving your body as you admire the scenery around you, feeling so light and free.

Enjoy the peace that being in your own company brings and allow your thoughts to drift to how life has been for you recently and to something you have been struggling to accept. Spend a moment allowing whatever comes to mind to arrive. Welcome it. Spend time with it. Explore it. Allow it. Allow, too, any sensations that arrive alongside it. There is nothing to resist or to alter here, there is nothing to force. All you need to do is to be here, in this moment, engaging with whatever has arrived for you as best you can.

As you continue along the forest path, consider what it would be like to offer whatever has arrived for you, and the part of you that has been struggling with it, compassion, kindness and gratitude. Connect with yourself in this way as deeply as you can, perhaps by offering yourself some kind words, such as, 'For so long I pushed against this and turned my back on it, but now I see it, I accept it, I allow it.' Only go as far with this as you feel able to. There is nothing to force, rather an acceptance of what is, as much as you feel able to in this moment.

If you are experiencing any sensations during this process and these sensations have arrived in a part of your body that you can lay your hands on, go ahead and do so, sending love and acceptance to these sensations. This love and acceptance can take the form of an energy or intention that passes from your heart to your hands, to this chosen part of you. Or it could take the form of a bright healing light, or perhaps a particular colour or form that naturally arrives for you. Take your time in this moment of connection. There is nothing to force or to rush. This is your time and your gift to yourself.

As you walk deeper into the forest you suddenly hear the sound of water in the distance. With each step you feel yourself getting closer to the water and, as you round the corner, you see a clearing in the trees up ahead and a tranquil, glistening river. A picturesque lookout point awaits beside this river in the form of a large, smooth rock. It's like a chair, waiting for you to rest upon it.

The rock is placed perfectly, high up on this vantage point, and you sit on this rock and look out at the water in front of you.

You feel so comfortable and at ease in this moment. You feel enveloped in a deep sense of acceptance that you are surprised has arrived for you.

As you sit on this rock, suddenly you hear gentle footsteps behind you and, without turning, your soul recognises the person who is walking to meet you. It is someone you feel very safe with. You smile as they get closer and make space for them to sit down beside you. They look at you as they sit and give you a gentle, warm, comforting hug. You feel so safe and at peace sitting beside them, taking in the beauty of your surroundings.

You talk for a while, pouring out everything you want to say. Everything you need to say. Everything you've been carrying. Take as long as you need here in this special moment, saying everything you need to and soaking in their presence beside you in this beautiful setting.

Once you've said everything you feel compelled to, feeling so much lighter in the process, they respond gently, but powerfully, telling you everything you need to hear. Listen to their wisdom. Feel the acceptance and peace that arrives for you in this moment. You met here for a reason.

When the time feels right, you both stand and hug each other goodbye. You turn and begin your journey home, feeling the warm sun on your back and the lightness in your shoulders. You feel so relaxed. So calm. So at peace. Enjoy the sights, sounds and smells of the forest around you as you make your journey back.

Before too long you find yourself back at the point of the forest you entered and before you leave, you turn to look back on your journey and smile because of all it has offered you.

When you are ready to leave this peaceful place, slowly begin to reawaken your body. Know that you can return to this forest in your imagination whenever you like. As you reawaken, keep with you the feeling of calm, peace, relaxation and acceptance.

Be very gentle with yourself as you transition from this healing exercise back to your day. Allow any realisations that may have arrived to stay with you as you arrive back in the external world, perhaps taking a few moments to write down anything that came up for you that you would like to hold on to and remember, or that you would like to release. Go gently and go slowly. This is deep and powerful work that is transformative on many levels.

As we near the end of Step Ten Accept What Is, and the journey we have experienced together throughout this deeply healing experience, I invite you to engage in two final healing exercises that will strengthen and support you as you embrace who you are, and the pillars that surround your life. I hope these exercises are as powerful for you as I know them to be, and that you can embrace them and all that they possess.

INNER CHILD HEALING EXERCISE FOR SELF-ACCEPTANCE

Find a space and time where you can connect with your inner child as deeply as possible. Create the best environment to facilitate this, perhaps burning some incense, essential oils or candles, playing some soft soothing music, and gathering everything you will need for this journey. When you are ready, settle in for a deeply healing experience.

For this exercise, you can connect with your inner child by calling them to your mind's eye as vividly as you can, or by writing them a letter. It may help you to go back to Step Four Heal Your Inner Child and complete the second healing exercise, where you will connect very deeply with your inner child in their entirety. The aim of this healing exercise, however you choose to practise it, is to connect with this younger version of you, in whatever way they arrive, and once you have made this connection with them and sat with it for a while, to shower them with love and acceptance of every single part of them. Their eyes, their hair, their perfect little fingers and toes, their innocent facial expressions, their personality traits and their talents, their heart and soul and way of showing up in the world, their quirks and all the special parts of them that are unique and perfectly imperfect exactly as they are. Shower them in unconditional love, acceptance and affirmation in the way you may have once wished to receive. In the way that you may have once yearned for from another, but that you can now offer yourself. For you (and the inner child you carry within) are so precious and so perfect, exactly as you are.

To take this exercise a step further, something you may feel ready to do in this moment, or perhaps when you've completed this exercise a number of times (as I would encourage you to do, as with many of the other exercises in these ten healing steps), is to take the love and acceptance you have showered upon your inner child, and to offer it now to yourself. This may feel extremely unfamiliar and like unchartered waters, but, as best you can, and as vividly as you can, whether through a visualisation, letter or journal exercise, offer this love and acceptance to yourself, in the belief that it will penetrate and sink in, for it will.

Come back to this exercise as often as you can. Repeating it will be incredibly powerful and transformative, and will lead you towards self-acceptance and unconditional love in a way you have never before experienced.

Now I offer you the final healing exercise of our ten-step journey together. An exercise that will support you hugely in loving and accepting yourself exactly as you are. Engage in this exercise over the next 21 days, and embrace it, and yourself, in all the power that ensues.

POSITIVE AFFIRMATIONS HEALING EXERCISE

As we learned in Step Five Silence Your Inner Critic and Step Six Strengthen Self-Compassion, a really powerful way to work towards deep inner healing is through the introduction of positive affirmations into your life. This extends to the process of acceptance too, so along your acceptance and self-acceptance journey I invite you to complete this positive affirmation healing exercise every day for 21 days, using five of the suggested affirmations below or choosing your own. To bring this healing exercise to an even deeper level, practise in front of a mirror, and soak yourself in as you repeat these powerful words to yourself.

To begin, take a deep breath and recite out loud your chosen affirmations slowly and clearly. Allow yourself to absorb the positive energy of the words you are repeating to yourself as best you can. Repeat each affirmation three times:

Everything is unfolding exactly as it should, including my growth and development.

I accept and love myself and my life unconditionally.

Today I will practise patience and loving kindness to myself and to every one and every situation I encounter.

I release all doubt and insecurity I once carried about myself. I am whole and perfect, exactly as I am.

I love and believe in the person who lives in my body and carries me through the day.

I am strong and healthy and can take good care of myself.

I am worthy of my own love and affection. I am enough exactly as I am.

I walk peacefully into the day trusting myself with all that comes my way.

I am worthy of joy and happiness and love.

I let go of judgement and fill the empty space with love, compassion and understanding.

I am a unique gift to this world and delight in sharing this gift.

I accept all things and all parts of myself exactly as they are.

I accept and release everything in my life that is beyond my power to change.

I accept life without judgement or criticism.

I accept myself and others completely and unconditionally.

I hope the above healing exercise offers you as much as does for me and the wonderful clients I work with. Come back to this exercise, and the ones that have come before it, as many times as you feel called to, for it is my deepest hope that they help you to 'accept who you are; and revel in it' (Mitch Albom).

STEP TEN ACCEPT WHAT IS SUMMARY

For so long I pushed and pulled against so many aspects of my life. My early experiences. My shyness and sensitivity. The relationships in my life that brought sadness and self-doubt. My body. My fear. I spent many hours wondering what I could do to make things different ... to make me different. It was only when I realised that it is not always possible (or necessary) to change the difficult things in life that a sense of ease arrived. An acceptance. Couple this with the beautiful power of self-compassion and the peace this brought into my life alongside my newfound experience of acceptance, and things drastically changed for me in so many ways. By journeying through Step Ten Accept What Is with me, alongside the previous steps we have visited together, my wish for you is that you too experience this change and the peace and serenity it brings. This is the work, this is the healing, and by giving yourself this gift you are transforming your life and healing yourself in ways you might never have thought were possible. Bravo!

CONCLUSION

WRAP YOURSELF IN GENTLE WORDS
(MY PARTING WORDS FROM MY HEART TO YOURS)

Wrap yourself in gentle words
In love and warmth and light
For you are safe, my love
With no more fires to fight

For years you've battled with yourself
And the demons at your door
But it's time for you to rest, my love
Safe in the knowledge of all you are

For peace has always been within
In your body and in your heart
And it is time for you to surrender
And to trust in this fresh start

Because everything you've ever yearned for
is within you, close at reach
And you are so deserving
of allowing this inner peace

So wrap yourself in gentle words
In love and warmth and light
And allowing yourself to surrender
And to trust in this fresh start

What a journey we have been on together. I have no doubt it has been full of ups and downs, smiles and tears, moments of deep inner peace and acceptance, but also periods of anger, frustration and immeasurable pain. As I shared in my opening words, 'this is the work, this is the healing', and healing, although the greatest gift you can offer yourself, is messy, tumultuous and incredibly difficult. So whether this journey has unfolded for you across one week, one month, or one year, I am so proud of you; for your bravery, your tenacity and the huge strength it has taken you to arrive here. I hope throughout your journey my words and the lessons I have learned from a lifetime of my own deep inner healing, combined with the years I have spent sitting across from others who bravely navigated their own, have offered you comfort, acceptance, true and meaningful transformation and the inner peace you have been yearning for, deep down, for so long now.

My hope for you is that you can take these learnings with you and offer them to yourself time and time again, through honouring your emotions and regulating your nervous system whenever you feel overwhelmed; connecting with your inner child when they need it most; silencing your inner critic and offering yourself the love, patience and compassion you so richly deserve; and strengthening your self-worth and how you perceive yourself. You are a beautiful soul who has so much to offer this world. I just hope that now you can finally begin to realise this, and that by allowing yourself to pause and come home to yourself, you can give yourself the powerful gift of connecting with your innate inner wisdom and healing the deep-rooted pain you have carried for so long.

I believe that our healing journeys are lifelong, so it is my hope that this book can become your bedside bible. One you reach for whenever you need a reminder of how to offer yourself exactly what you need in that moment. It might be a healing inner child meditation, a soothing somatic sequence, a reminder of how to offer yourself the compassion and love you so freely give to everyone else around you, or the ways in which you can calm anxiety and stress and guide yourself to peace, calm and tranquillity. I hope too that you can give yourself the time and space you need to truly incorporate *The Steps*. If there are any healing exercises or passages you feel compelled to revisit, whether now or in the future, please do. Revisit them time and again, and in doing so strengthen the power and deep healing they have to offer you. You are on a continual journey, one that has so much to offer you, your inner peace, and your happiness and fulfilment in life.

Go gently and with hope in your heart, for this work works and the key to deep and lasting transformation is now in your hands.

> I wish you so much love and light,
> Clodagh x

MENTAL HEALTH SUPPORT SERVICES

- Your GP is a fantastic first step when it comes to seeking support for your mental health

- The HSE National Counselling Service is available across Ireland and is free of charge to those who experienced childhood abuse or neglect, are former residents of a mother and baby home, are a family member impacted by the Stardust inquest or have a medical card.

- turn2me provides free online counselling and online support groups for young people aged 12 to 17 and adults
www.turn2me.ie

- Aware are a national organisation that provide free support, education and information services to people impacted by anxiety, depression, bipolar disorder and related mood conditions
www.aware.ie

- Samaritans provide confidential, non-judgemental emotional support, 24 hours a day for people who are experiencing feelings of distress or despair
Phone helpline: 116 123   Email: jo@samaritans.ie
Website: www.samaritans.org/ireland

- Shine provide support services for people living with mental health difficulties and their families
www.shine.ie

- To find a psychologist visit the Psychological Society of Ireland website
www.psychologicalsociety.ie

- To find a counsellor or psychotherapist visit the Irish Association for Counselling and Psychotherapy website
www.iacp.ie

SELECT BIBLIOGRAPHY

American Psychological Association (2018). *APA Dictionary of Psychology*. [online] APA Dictionary of Psychology. https://dictionary.apa.org/.

American Psychological Association (2022). 'Control anger before it controls you.' *American Psychological Association.* [online] https://www.apa.org/topics/anger/control.

Carroll, Anna. (2014). *The Feedback Imperative: How to Give Everyday Feedback to Speed Up Your Team's Success.* Austin, Texas: River Grove Books.

Hibbert, Dr Christina. (2013) *This Is How We Grow: A Psychologist's Memoir of Loss, Motherhood, & Discovering Self-Worth & Joy, One Season at a Time.* USA: Oracle Folio Books.

Waldinger, Robert J. and Schulz, Mark. (2010). *The Harvard Study of Adult Development.* [online] https://www.adultdevelopmentstudy.org/.

ACKNOWLEDGEMENTS

ACKNOWLEDGEMENTS

When I was a little girl, my mum gave me the greatest gift: my love of reading. She taught me that 'as long as you can read, you will never feel alone', and this sentiment so closely matches why my soul so strongly desired to bring *The Steps* into the world: to help others feel less alone. To help *you* feel less alone. Thank you, dear reader, for trusting me to guide you along this healing journey. My heart is so full, knowing you have held this book in your hands and taken in my words. I hope you received everything you desired, and more, from this experience, and that *The Steps* becomes your bedside bible that you reach for time and again, especially when you need it most.

To my wonderful Instagram and *Unspoken* community, without whom *The Steps* would never have been born. I never imagined when I pressed 'publish' on my first Instagram post and podcast episode that I would receive in such abundance everything I have from you all: love, kindness, encouragement, gratitude and so much more. My confidence has grown so much since those early days, because of you. Thank you, thank you, thank you.

A very special thank you to the incredible clients I have had the privilege of working with since beginning my career as a psychologist. You have taught me so much and inspired me in so many ways. I am in awe of you and think of every single one of you often. I will forever hold you and our relationships in my heart.

To my mentors, therapists, teachers and energy healers. My growth and inner peace are thanks to you. I never thought I would reach a place of such contentment and calm, and for this I thank you profoundly. My life has changed because of you.

Thank you to my wonderful agency, 84 World, for all the help they have provided me along the way, most especially in bringing *The Steps* to life. I would be lost without my incredible agent and friend, Michele McGrath, who has held my hand step by step (excuse the pun!) and believed in me from the very beginning. How lucky I am that the stars aligned to bring us together. *The Steps* would not have been brought into the world without you, and for that I will be eternally grateful.

Thank you so much to the team at Gill Books. I count myself so lucky to be part of the Gill family and from the moment our work together began I could see how clearly you all 'got me'. I felt so heard, so supported and so encouraged while working with you, and it has been a privilege to watch *The Steps* grow and evolve under your guidance. A special thank you to my Publisher, Sarah Liddy, who was an absolute delight to work with (and very patient!); my editor, Aoife Harrison, who has the most profound knowledge and understanding of the English language and who guided me so kindly through the process; and to Charlie Lawlor, Kristen Olson and Graham Thew for their expertise, talent and kindness.

To Donna Ashworth, someone I admire so much and whom I had the pleasure of meeting recently. Thank you for allowing me to borrow 'Your Light'. Your beautiful words inspire me so much and I feel very privileged to share some of them as part of *The Steps.*

A huge thank you to the gorgeous group of soul sisters I am lucky enough to call my friends. I count myself so fortunate to have so many cheerleaders and forever friends in my life. We've been through thick and thin together, and life would not be the same without you. You know who you are, and I am so blessed to have you in my life. I love you all dearly.

Mum, where do I begin? I have always felt so loved and so special in your eyes. To have had someone I could always be my authentic self with has been the greatest gift in life, and to know so deeply that if I ever needed you, you would be there in a heartbeat, has gotten me through so much. Thank you for everything. For loving me. For raising me. For teaching me all of life's most important lessons. I love you.

To my dad, whom I miss every single day. Thank you for being my rock, my comfort and my security. I feel you with me always and know how proud you are of me. How lucky I was to have had such an incredible father.

To my wider family, thank you for everything. How blessed I was to grow up with so many people surrounding me and where every door was always open.

To my Campbell family, thank you for welcoming me into your lives with so much love and acceptance. I feel so at home with you all and so lucky to have such a kind and caring circle around me.

Paul, my soulmate and greatest life decision. Thank you for loving and accepting me so wholly, exactly as I am, and for your constant patience, compassion, sensitivity, generosity and consideration. Life is such an adventure by your side, and I am so grateful for all you do for me and our beautiful family. I thank my lucky stars for you every single day and would be lost without you. I love you so much.

To my precious daughters, Maia, Lulu and Emmie. You are my greatest and most precious gift in life. I adore you and feel so lucky to be your mama. I never thought I would experience love like the love you have brought into my life. You are such wise and perfect little souls and offer so much joy to everyone you cross paths with, especially me. I am so proud of you and can't wait to experience what's ahead. I love you to the moon and back.